Dear Friend of the Radio Bible Class:

Please accept this volume as an expression of our appreciation for your past interest and help in keeping the broadcast of the Class on the air, sending the Gospel message to the ends of the earth.

MR DeHaan

Deuteronomy 29:29

Dear Doctor:
I have a problem

Dear Doctor:
I have a problem

Answers to Bible Questions
VOLUME TWO

by

M. R. DE HAAN, M.D.

RADIO BIBLE CLASS
GRAND RAPIDS, MICHIGAN

Printed in the United States of America

DEDICATION

To the thousands of interested listeners to the Radio Bible Class who have sent in the various questions contained in this volume, and whose interest in things spiritual has been a source of great encouragement, this second volume of Bible Questions and Answers is gratefully and prayerfully dedicated.

INTRODUCTION

The first volume of Answers to Bible Questions was published in 1952 under the title, "508 Answers to Bible Questions." The immediate and enthusiastic response to this volume, and the sustained interest it has enjoyed, very soon made it evident that a real need had been met. The volume of testimonies received both in the mail and by mouth, soon convinced us that a second similar volume containing a new set of Bible questions was desirable. This conviction prompted us to begin gathering new and different material over the past eight years since the appearance of "508 Answers to Bible Questions."

As in the previous volume, the contents very largely consists of questions sent in by listeners to the RADIO BIBLE CLASS over the years, and the answers to these questions as dictated by the writer of this volume. Two aims have been kept in sharp focus in selecting the questions from the thousands of others. These aims were: (1) Questions most frequently asked, and therefore indicating the greatest need in the minds of the listeners; and (2) Answers which would prove most helpful and of greatest importance and interest to the largest number of readers. Many of the questions in this volume were asked at various times by hundreds of different listeners, independently of each other, and therefore represent those questions uppermost in the minds of many people.

Again, as in the first book of this type, most of the credit for its preparation is due Miss Leona Hertel, the author's secretary for almost twenty years. As she transcribed the answers dictated, she kept copies of all those on important subjects, indexing and collating the material by subject and Scripture reference. This practice was begun long before we had any intention of publishing them. The paragraphs were recorded first of all for use by our office personnel. Since many of the questions were "repeats," the answers were filed alphabetically and by Scripture in loose-leaf volumes for office reference; so that once the question had been answered, the same answer could be given to all others who later asked the same question concerning the same subject or passage of Scripture. This eliminated the herculean task of having to dictate an answer to the same question repeatedly. Instead, the one answering the problem could turn to this book of authentic answers and merely "quote" what had been dictated before, relating to the same problem.

When it was later decided to publish a book on Bible Answers to Questions, this file proved to be of inestimable value, for in it was a wealth of material sufficient not for one single volume but many volumes.

The questions in this book as in the former one, have been painstakingly selected from this mass of available questions and answers on the basis of expressed interest, and relative importance. Questions of a local, temporary, or personal nature have been carefully avoided and left out. If the response to our first volume is any indication of the blessings which will attend this newest number, we know it will reward us for all the meticulous care which has gone into its preparation.

We send forth this new compilation of material, encouraged by the promise of God's blessing, and with the prayer that multitudes may find in these pages not only answers to satisfy their curiosity, but answers which will lift burdens, comfort hearts, and bring salvation and assurance.

M. R. DE HAAN, M.D.

CONTENTS

CHAPTER I

THE BIBLE

1. You stated that we shall keep on studying the Word even after we get to Heaven. This is the first time I have ever heard this statement, and I would like to know on what it is based.

Concerning the fact that we shall continue to study the Word after we get to Heaven, I do not know any statement in the Word of God that says this in just so many words. However, we believe that since the Word of God is the written expression of the living Word of God, the Lord Jesus Christ, and He is infinite in all His attributes, that we shall never be able to exhaust the Scriptures. I believe that it is this that the Lord Jesus Christ meant when He said:

> Heaven and earth shall pass away, but my words shall not pass away (Matt. 24:35).

And again in the Psalms:

> For ever, O LORD, thy word is settled in heaven (Ps. 119:89).

As a revelation of Almighty God, I believe that the Bible is as limitless and infinite in its teaching as the Author Himself. This is why it is called a "living word" and will endure forever, and I am convinced in my own mind that we shall always continue to find new treasures in this wonderful Book.

Please do not misunderstand me. I am not dogmatic about the thing, and wouldn't start a new denomination on this theory; but if I am wrong, we shall find out, of course, when we get to glory, and I shall be most happy to admit my mistake. Many of these things are not clear now, but then "we shall know as we are known."

2. I have been using the Moffatt translation in my Bible study, and have become confused in my understanding of certain passages. I am a young Christian and perhaps I have not been using the right method of study. Can you help me?

In regard to the problem which you stated in your letter, I am sorry to say that many of the modern translations come far short of what they ought to be. While I believe that some of them are helpful to mature Christians, I do not believe that they ought to be used by new converts, and those who may be easily carried away and swayed by these translations. Moffatt's is not a safe translation, and I believe personally that there has been no better translation made than the King James Version. I would advise you to stick by it. If you do not own a Scofield edition of the King James Version, I would recommend that you secure one, and use it above all others. The notes in this Bible are very, very helpful, and the translation, of course, is the old, accepted one which has stood for all these years. I am sure that prayerful study from this Bible will clear up the confusion you have had, and aid you in a clearer understanding of God's Word.

3. Can you give me any information on the book of "Jasher" mentioned in II Samuel 1:18 and Joshua 10:13?

(Also he bade them teach the children of Judah the use of the bow: behold, it is written in the *book of Jasher*) (II Sam. 1:18).

> And the sun stood still, and the moon stayed, until the
> people had avenged themselves upon their enemies. Is
> not this written in the *book of Jasher?* (Josh. 10:13).

It is usually understood that it was a book of songs or
hymns which were written early in the history of the
children of Israel. However, we do not believe that it
was an inspired book, such as the rest of the books of the
Bible, and therefore is not included in the canon of Scripture. It was one of the many historical books in existence
at the time containing interesting facts to which even the
writers of the Scripture referred, but is not considered to
be one of the books of the Bible.

4. How can you claim the Bible to be a scientific book when it says there was light before the sun was created?

Science today has proven there is light wholly independent of the sun. All matter radiates invisible light.
Radium, phosphorous, and other elements emanate light.
The light of the firefly and the glowworm has never been
explained. Light was given to the sun on the fourth day
of creation, but light was present on the first day.

5. We have heard many reports pro and con concerning the Revised Standard Version of the Bible, and would like your opinion concerning using this version for study.

Concerning the *New Revised Standard Version* of the
Bible, I reject it completely because of two reasons. First
of all, I reject it because of those who are backing its pro-
motion. As you will see from the flyleaf of the book, it is
being put out by the National Council of Churches, and I
want nothing to do with that group whatsoever.

Secondly, they have made a number of changes in the
text which I think are exceedingly dangerous. One of
them is in Isaiah 7, where they have changed the word

"virgin" to "young woman." Another one is Matthew 27:54 where the definite article "the" has been changed to the indefinite article "a," so that it reads, "Truly this was A son of God."

I believe that these little subtle changes, and there are a great many more, make it an unsafe book to recommend to others. I think the best thing for us to do is to stick by the old King James version, and especially the Scofield Reference Bible edition. Nothing better has yet been produced. I certainly would not recommend the *New Revised Standard Version* to the average individual.

6. **Why is Acts 8:37 left out of the Revised Standard Version of the Bible? It is in the King James Version, and I read in Revelation 22:18, 19 about adding to or taking away from the Word of God.**

The omission of Acts 8:37 from the Revised Standard Version is only one example of the many violations which this translation does to the Word of God. Personally, I have no use whatsoever for these new editions which tell us that certain portions are not in the original manuscripts. It is much safer to stay by the King James Version which at least was not translated by modernists and unbelievers. We believe that these things are also a sign of the times.

7. **How can you say the Bible is infallible, when it contradicts itself? For instance, Matthew and Luke give entirely different genealogies of Jesus.**

Matthew and Luke do not contradict each other, but are in perfect harmony. Matthew traces the genealogy of Joseph (the foster-father of Jesus) from David through Solomon, the son of David. Luke, however, traces the

genealogy of Mary who was also a descendant of David —
not through Solomon but through Solomon's brother
Nathan. Compare Matthew 1:6 (Solomon's line) with
Luke 3:31 (Nathan's line).

> And Jesse begat David the king; and David the king begat
> Solomon of her that had been the wife of Urias (Matt. 1:6).
> Which was the son of Melea, which was the son of Menan,
> which was the son of Mattatha, which was THE SON OF
> NATHAN, WHICH WAS THE SON OF DAVID (Luke
> 3:31).

In Matthew we have Christ as King; hence His ancestry
is traced only to Abraham, the father of the Kingdom
nation. But in Luke, Jesus is the son of MAN, and His
ancestry is carried back to Adam, the first human.

8. I have a friend who constantly asks for proof of the Scriptures. Is there some publication designed to show how the various branches of science harmonize with God's Word?

You must remember that the Scriptures do not have
to be proven, but they are to be accepted by faith. The
opening statement of the Bible is: "In the beginning God
created the heavens and the earth." There is no proof
given for this, and no details as to how or when or of what
material God did this. He expects us just to believe it and
accept it because it is God's Word. This, of course, is a
death blow to our pride, because we like to have proof and
to understand; but God's condition is that we shall accept
it because He says it, and not ask to understand things
which are beyond our comprehension.

However, there is sufficient evidence for the truth of
the Scriptures to the enlightened mind. To the natural
mind, of course, all of these things must remain a mystery,
but to those who have been enlightened by the Holy

Spirit, all nature and all creation attest to the truth of the existence of God, and the very history of the Word of God throughout all the centuries is its own verification and substantiation.

There are, however, a number of good books which have been written on the matter of science and the Bible. There is one by Dr. Harry Rimmer on "Science and the Scriptures" which you should be able to obtain through your local religious bookstore, or by ordering it through the Zondervan Publishing House, Grand Rapids, Michigan.

9. What is your opinion of the Amplified New Testament?

In recent years there has been a rash of many, many different translations and editions of the Bible. It seems to have become a fad for somebody to give a new version of the Bible, and in most cases it is just the opinion of another individual. Other translations are helpful for personal study, but I do not believe that they should be used in place of the King James Version. I have a copy of the Amplified New Testament on my desk, and refer to it from time to time. In many instances it does give a clear explanation, but I still believe that the King James Version is the best translation. There are so many different versions on the market today, that many people are becoming utterly confused.

10. Would you recommend the use of the Phillips Translation of the Bible?

I can only recommend it for private use, and for personal study, but do not recommend it for public use in meetings. The different translations may be helpful for one's personal home study, but I do believe that the King James Version is still the best to use for public worship.

11. What do you think about the new revision of the Scofield Bible Notes?

I have not yet seen the new revision of the "Scofield Bible Notes." While the proposed revision is disturbing to some of us, the purpose behind it, however, is clear. The present edition, copyrighted in 1909 and copyright renewed in 1937, will become public domain in 1965. After this expiration date, the Scofield Bible Notes can be printed and reproduced by anyone without infringement. The publisher, therefore, desires a revision so that a new copyright may be secured.

CHAPTER II

BIBLE PERSONALITIES

12. Did Adam and Eve have other children, and who did their sons marry?

The Bible does not tell us how many children Adam and Eve had. However, in Genesis 5:4 we are told that after the birth of Seth, Adam and Eve became the parents of additional sons and daughters. How many, we do not know, but it is generally assumed that Cain and Seth must have married their sisters, and from this the race began.

You must remember there was no objection to brothers and sisters marrying at that time, because the race had not yet completely degenerated to the place where it is today. I think that this is the correct answer, and it is one of those things that we will know more fully when we meet the Lord Jesus Christ at His coming.

13. Before the fall, did Adam and Eve see the Lord personally?

Concerning whether Adam and Eve ever saw God personally, we do not believe that any man ever saw God personally, but that He has appeared to people in human form in Christophanies and theophanies. However, no man can see God face to face and live.

And he said, Thou canst not see my face: for there shall no man see me, and live (Ex. 33:20).

14. How many wives did Abraham have during his lifetime?

The Bible mentions only three by name, but Abraham had other wives called "concubines" whose names are not given (Gen. 25:5, 6). His first wife was Sarah; his second was Hagar; and after Sarah died, he married again, and raised a large family (Gen. 25:1-4). The third wife's name was Keturah.

15. I heard you say on the air that Abraham was not an Israelite, and Jacob was not a Jew. Did I hear you correctly? Will you please explain?

Abraham was the first man ever called a Hebrew (Gen. 14:13). The word "Hebrew" means "one who crossed over." As such his descendants were called Hebrews. Jacob was the first Israelite, when his name was changed (Gen. 32:28). The name "Jew" was applied to members of the Southern Kingdom of Judah, and means a "Judahite." Abraham then was a Hebrew; Jacob was both a Hebrew and an Israelite, and a Jew is also a Hebrew and an Israelite.

16. My pastor read in one of your books that Cain and Abel were twins. Do you really believe this?

Yes, I believe they were, as a fulfillment of the "multiplied" conception pronounced upon the woman (Gen. 3:16).

> Unto the woman he said, I will greatly multiply thy sorrow and thy conception (Gen. 3:16).

Genesis 4:1, 2 mentions only ONE conception, but TWO births. The verse can be translated:

> And she continued to bare his brother Abel (Gen. 4:2).

17. Since there were no women in the world at that time, who did Cain marry?

Cain married one of his sisters. Genesis 5:4 informs us that Adam was the father of daughters, besides additional sons:

> And the days of Adam after he had begotten Seth were eight hundred years: AND HE BEGAT SONS AND DAUGHTERS (Gen. 5:4).

18. Was Caiaphas the high priest a saved man?

> And one of them, named Caiaphas, being the high priest that same year, said unto them, Ye know nothing at all,
> Nor consider that it is expedient for us, that one man should die for the people, and that the whole nation perish not.
> And this spake he not of himself: but being high priest that year, he prophesied that Jesus should die for that nation;
> And not for that nation only, but that also he should gather together in one of the children of God that were scattered abroad (John 11:49-52).

I do not believe that Caiaphas the high priest was a saved man. There is nothing in the Bible to indicate that he was. Some who suppose it, base it on the fact that he prophesied in the passages in John 11; but this was not unusual for him, on account of his office as high priest; it does not indicate that he was a saved man.

19. Why did David take five smooth stones when he needed only one to kill Goliath? Is this a type of any particular thing?

Concerning the five smooth stones which David took from the brook in preparation for his contest with Goliath, there have been many different interpretations given; but probably the most satisfactory one is that since

Goliath had four brothers, it is possible that David took enough stones to slay not only Goliath, but his four brothers as well. I do not know that David was a type of anyone in particular in this instance, although we do know that he was a type of the Lord Jesus Christ in his victory over our enemy, the Devil. Then too, we are to remember that FIVE is the number of grace, and it certainly was by the grace of God that David was able to overcome Goliath.

20. I heard a good fundamental preacher say that Esther was a harlot just as much as Rahab. I had never heard her spoken of in that way before, but always considered her a wonderful woman. He said that in Esther, Chapter 4, it showed her change of heart, and she was converted. Would you agree to this teaching?

I do not find that there is anything in the record of the Bible which either teaches or remotely suggests that Esther was a harlot. This is the interpretation which some teachers have placed on some obscure passages, but there is no basis for it in Scripture whatsoever. From the record in Esther there is no reason to believe but that she was a faithful and a pure young woman, and therefore the king chose her to be his bride. I certainly cannot agree with the interpretation that there was anything impure about Esther.

21. Do you think that Isaac was the age of 33 when Abraham offered him?

The age of Isaac when his father Abraham offered him is not stated in Scripture. Some people believe that in order to fulfill the type of the Lord Jesus Christ he was about 33 years old. I realize that there are other guesses but I do not believe that any of them can be stated with any positive certainty. What a wonderful thing it will be when we get to Heaven, and find out all about these things.

22. Why did Jacob (being a cheat) find favor with God?

Why God should show favor to Jacob in spite of the fact that he was a cheat, is because God dealt in grace with Jacob. He did not justify what Jacob did in the least, but God showed His mercy and sovereign grace by choosing Jacob in spite of, and not because of, his shortcomings. This is not only true of Jacob but of all of us, that we are saved not because God saw something good in us, but because of His matchless grace.

23. Was John the Baptist the same as Elias or Elijah?

According to the prophecy of Malachi, Elijah will return just before the Second Coming of the Lord Jesus Christ. He is described as one of the two witnesses in Revelation 11, and we believe that after the Church is gone, Elias (Elijah) and Moses will witness to the children of Israel. John the Baptist was the forerunner of the Lord Jesus Christ at His first coming, just as Elijah will be the forerunner of the Lord Jesus at His Second Coming. While they are not the same person, they do have the same functions, and if the Nation of Israel had accepted Christ at His first coming, it would have been Elijah who would have come, but since He knew that they would reject Him, He sent John the Baptist in the spirit of Elijah, and therefore Jesus said, "Elias indeed is come." John was to the first coming what Elijah will be to the Second Coming — the King's herald.

24. Was Judas Iscariot present when the Lord's Supper was instituted?

Judas Iscariot was NOT present at the Lord's Supper

on the evening when Christ ordained this ordinance. Apparently from the Gospel records, he was there when they celebrated the Passover feast, and then left between the Passover feast and the institution of the Lord's Supper.

25. Is there any special significance in Judas' committing suicide?

I believe the only significance we can attach to the fact that Judas committed suicide was that when the Devil was through with him, he destroyed him. There is no question in my mind but that Judas was the Devil-man, and was possessed of the Devil in his betrayal of the Lord; being used by the Devil for this purpose, when the Devil was through with him, he destroyed him, as he always does with those who are subject to his will. Personally, I believe that the first attempt of Satan to produce a personal Antichrist was Judas, and that there is a great possibility that Judas will be resurrected after the Rapture of the Church to become the personal Antichrist of the latter days. Of course, this is a personal opinion, but I believe that there is much of Scripture to support this view.

26. Was Lot a saved man when he fled from Sodom?

Yes, the Bible definitely teaches Lot was saved — saved "so as by fire." (See II Peter 2:7, 8).

> And delivered just Lot, vexed with the filthy conversation of the wicked.
>
> (For that righteous man dwelling among them, in seeing and hearing, vexed his righteous soul from day to day with their unlawful deeds) (II Pet. 2:7, 8).

27. Did Manasseh take the place of Dan?

I believe that because the Antichrist is to come out of the tribe of Dan that the Lord has omitted Dan in the blessing of the future, and instead has substituted Manasseh.

28. Was Matthias or Paul chosen to replace Judas?

I have looked at both sides of this situation, and I am personally convinced that Matthias was a choice of the flesh, and not the leading of the Spirit. He is not spoken of again after being chosen by the disciples. The fact that Nathaniel, Andrew, and others are not mentioned is not significant, because they are sufficiently mentioned before this incident in Acts, chapter 1.

However, though we may differ in our opinions here below, we shall know all the truth when we stand before the Lord.

29. Why were Moses and Aaron not permitted to enter the Land of Canaan?

There are different interpretations as to why the Lord forbade Moses and Aaron to enter the Land of Canaan, and it is usually supposed that it was because they smote the rock. However, I believe that Moses had in his hand the rod of Aaron (cf. Num. 17:10 and Num. 20:8), and not his own rod at the time. They were disobedient; Moses should have SPOKEN to the rock instead of smiting it. There are many different opinions in regard to this matter, and I believe that the best we can do is wait until we have more light before becoming dogmatic.

30. Why did the Egyptians seek to kill Moses when he was a baby, and not his older brother Aaron?

The reason that Aaron did not perish, undoubtedly was because the decree of Pharaoh had not yet been issued at the time of Aaron's birth.

31. How long was Noah in the Ark?

Concerning the length of Noah's stay in the Ark, if you will read carefully Genesis 7:11, you will find the day on which Noah entered into the Ark, which was the second month, and the seventeenth day of the month. Then if you will turn to the eighth chapter of Genesis, you will find in the second month, on the seven and twentieth day, of the next year, Noah was commanded to go out of the Ark. This would mean that Noah was in the Ark one year and ten days.

32. We had a discussion in Sunday School about Noah's Ark, and one man said it was not a real story because the Ark could never have held all the animals and the loads of food necessary to keep them for months. I could not answer him. Can you help me?

The Ark, according to the Bible, was 450 feet long, 75 feet wide, and 45 feet high. This would mean a space of 1,518,750 cubic feet. This would be more than enough when you remember that only two of each kind (seven of a few for sacrifice) went in. There are many "kinds" of breeds of animals, but they belonged to the same family, and developed from a single species. Hence only two dogs went in (not two of every sub species or breed). Two mice would be enough (not two of every kind of mouse).

There are endless varieties of animals today as a result of mutation and cross-breeding, but the actual families from which they developed are not too many to be accommodated easily in the Ark. God knew exactly how much space was needed.

33. Was Paul the Apostle married?

We do not know whether Paul was married or not.

There are those who believe that Paul was a bachelor, while there are others who seem to believe that he might have been a widower. In any case, the Bible does not say definitely, and we will have to wait till we get to glory to know for sure.

34. Was the Apostle Paul acquainted with Jesus?

As to whether Paul was acquainted with Jesus when He was here on the earth, we cannot give a positive answer, although it does appear from II Corinthians 5:16 that Paul had met the Lord Jesus Christ:

> Wherefore henceforth know we no man after the flesh; yea, though we have known Christ after the flesh, yet now henceforth know we him no more (II Cor. 5:16).

If the expression in this verse means that he had seen Him in the flesh; that is, in person, then of course, it would mean that he had known Him. However, I do not believe that we can build a doctrine upon just one text, and therefore it remains a question as to whether this refers to Paul's actual acquaintance with Him or not.

35. We had a discussion concerning the death of both Paul and Peter. How did they both die?

The Bible has nothing definite to say about Paul's or Peter's death, and therefore it is mere speculation. We will have to wait to find out about this definitely until we get to Glory. Of course, there are traditions which say that Paul was beheaded, and that Peter was crucified upside down, but there is no Bible basis for this. It is only tradition.

36. Was Saul of Tarsus converted on the Damascus Road, or when Ananias laid hands upon him?

In regard to the date of the conversion of Saul, I do not

think that we can be absolutely sure. There are those who believe that he was born again when Ananias laid hands upon him, and others believe that he was converted when he caught the vision on the Damascus road. It is one of those things we may have to wait for until we get to Heaven. My personal opinion is that he was converted on the road to Damascus.

37. Was Samson saved?

Yes, Samson was a saved man, and is mentioned in the register of the heroes of the faith.

> And what shall I more say? for the time would fail me to tell of Gedeon, and of Barak, and of SAMSON, and of Jephthae; of David also, and Samuel, and of the prophets (Heb. 11:32).

38. Was Solomon a colored man? According to Song of Solomon 1:5, 6 it would seem that he was.

> I am black, but comely, O ye daughters of Jerusalem, as the tents of Kedar, as the curtains of Solomon.
> Look not upon me, because I am black, because the sun hath looked upon me (S. of Sol. 1:5, 6).

We cannot base any definite conclusion upon this passage. The Song of Solomon is a highly picturesque and symbolical love story which I believe is a poetic account of the love between the bridegroom and the bride. However, I do not believe that we can conclude that Solomon was a colored man. The tradition, of course, comes from the fact that it is taught in certain circles that Solomon was the offspring of a union between David and the Queen of Sheba. However, this is mere tradition and has no foundation in the Scriptures. The Bible clearly states that Solomon was the child of Bathsheba and not the Queen of Sheba.

CHAPTER III

THE BLOOD

39. If "flesh and blood" cannot inherit the Kingdom of Heaven, I cannot understand how our resurrected bodies will be visible and like Christ's when He ascended.

The expression "flesh and blood" occurs in I Corinthians 15:50,

> Now this I say, brethren, that flesh and blood cannot inherit the kingdom of God; neither doth corruption inherit incorruption (I Cor. 15:50).

You must remember that this is a Bible term used to express the old, Adamic nature, and has nothing to do with literal flesh and blood. It is merely the Bible way of saying that the old, Adamic nature shall never inherit the Kingdom of Heaven.

In regard to the body of the Lord Jesus, you must remember that after His resurrection, according to the closing chapter of Luke, Jesus had a body of flesh and of bone. In this body He ascended into Heaven, and with this body He of course will also return. He demonstrated that He was a body of flesh and of bone by eating with His disciples, which was the proof of His humanity and His bodily resurrection.

40. I have been ill, but do not feel that I can accept a blood transfusion, since the blood used might be that of a very sinful, degraded person, and I fear it would affect my life. Can you help me in this?

I can appreciate and understand your position. However, you must remember that when blood is taken for transfusion, it is taken only from healthy patients, and no blood from sick people or those who have apparent disease is ever used. The fact that a man has led a wicked life does not in any sense affect the quality or the potency of the blood, so that argument does not hold at all. I do not believe that we ought to be afraid, in the light of all that science has accomplished, to accept blood which has been properly typed and properly treated. There is absolutely no danger of transmitting any moral character or vicious tendency through the transfusion of the blood.

41. In a discussion in our Sunday School class the question came up as to whether there is any difference in the human blood and that of an animal. Can you help us?

Human blood and animal blood ARE NOT the same. God breathed life into Adam, but not into animals, and therefore an animal has a soul but no spirit.

42. I cannot understand how sin is in the blood stream. I have been taught that we are sinners by nature. Please set me right in this.

The full understanding of how the sin is transmitted from Adam to all of his offspring, of course, will remain more or less of a mystery until we see the Lord Jesus face to face. However, since life is in the blood, and life *is* the blood, and the wages of sin is death, therefore, the curse of Adam must be transmitted through the blood. In the Bible, "the blood of man" and "the sinful nature" are used interchangeably. The expression, for instance, "flesh and blood," is the Bible way of speaking of our sinful nature. So there is no conflict at all in saying that the sinful nature of Adam is transmitted through the blood, as well as through his old nature and the flesh.

43. **I read an article in the newspaper concerning a family who refused to allow their child to have a blood transfusion because of their religious belief. They said that the Bible prohibited the eating of blood, and that blood transfusions were the same as eating the blood. As a result of their refusal, their child died. Don't you think they should have permitted their child a chance to live?**

I do not believe that the prohibitions given in Genesis, Leviticus, and Deuteronomy against the eating of blood have anything to do with blood transfusions whatsoever. It has definitely been established that blood transfusions are one of the greatest lifesavers of today, and the stand of some people against it (for example, Jehovah's Witnesses) is not based upon a sound interpretation of Scripture. I realize that they are very difficult to deal with because they specialize on certain lines of argument, and it is very seldom that one is truly convinced. I believe that the only thing that you can do is to insist upon the fact that EATING BLOOD and receiving a transfusion are two quite different matters.

Chapter IV

CHRIST — QUESTIONS CONCERNING

44. I was talking with some people who said that Christ was not Deity while he was here on earth, but only a man. I would like to have a better understanding of this.

Undoubtedly you have been in touch with either the Jehovah's Witnesses or certain groups of Adventists who hold to these theories. However, it is absolutely impossible for a person to believe that Christ was only a man while He was here on earth, and still be a Christian believer. The first three verses of John 1 are enough to settle the Deity of Christ while He was here on earth. You will recall that this gospel opens with:

> In the beginning was the Word, and the Word was with God, and the Word was God.
> The same was in the beginning with God (John 1:1, 2).

Then in verse 14 of this same chapter we read:

> And the Word was made flesh, and dwelt among us, (and we beheld his glory, the glory as of the only begotten of the Father,) full of grace and truth (John 1:14).

This alone would establish the Deity of Christ. There are many, many other passages along this same line, and if I were you, I just would not listen to any of these folks

31

who come along with these strange theories, which are just another sign and indication of the deception of these latter days.

45. I heard you say that the "Father" did not forsake Christ on the Cross. How do you come to this conclusion?

Concerning the statement to which you refer that "the Father did not forsake Christ on the Cross," we must make a distinction between the relationship of Christ to God as Deity and the relationship to God as Father. As God, He did forsake His Son upon the Cross, and He had to suffer alone; but as Father, there is nothing in the Bible to indicate that He left Him in this way. I realize that this is a deep and involved question, but we can only go by that which has been revealed. The Lord Jesus Christ cried out, "My God, my God, why hast Thou forsaken Me?" but He did not use the expression, "My Father." We may be mistaken in this, but some day when we get to Glory, we shall understand and know completely.

46. Was the resurrection body of Christ the same as His body before He was crucified?

Concerning the body of the Lord Jesus Christ after His resurrection, you must remember that this was a spiritual body, not subject to the laws of nature. For this reason, He could pass through the door without opening it, go from one place to another in the twinkling of an eye, and also ascend up into Heaven against the laws of gravity.

However, in other respects the body was the same one which had been placed in the tomb. It was visible, recognizable, and tangible, and carried the scars of the nails in His hands; and so it was the same body, but a resurrection body. Our resurrection bodies will be like that too.

47. Why did our Lord have to descend from an adulterous source? It is made so vividly plain that David and Bathsheba were adulterers and yet it was the line of David through which it was necessary that Christ come. Why was not the line of David kept free of that taint? We do not understand the connection or the point of this part of the Scriptures.

I think that you will find the entire answer to this question in the fact of the "grace" of God. The Lord Jesus Christ in His wonderful, condescending love, identified Himself so completely with sinners that He was even willing to be born of a line that had been defiled not only by the sin of David and Bathsheba, but also way back in the days of Judah. This is an exhibition of God's wonderful grace, in that He could identify Himself with those who had fallen to the deepest depths, and yet not with any taint of sin. We believe this to be the result, of course, of the virgin birth, but it does exalt the grace of God, that it is not our worth, but only His grace that is able to save us.

48. What was the cause of Christ's death?

I believe the Bible is very, very clear that Jesus did not die from any physical cause, or even from crucifixion, but that He voluntarily laid down His life when the work was accomplished and done. The fact that water and blood came from the pierced side of our Saviour was only the proof that He was actually dead. After death the blood separates into the serum and the clot, and the fact that both of these came separately from the wound is the scientific evidence that He was really dead, and not merely in a swoon or a faint.

I do not believe that Christ died of a broken heart, or that He died from pain or agony. If you will read very, very carefully John 10:17, 18 I think you will find that the Lord Jesus voluntarily laid down His life after six hours, when the work was done. Certainly He did not die before the two thieves because He could not stand as much pain as they could, or because He was a weakling. He died by His own voluntary act when He knew that the work had been accomplished.

I believe that all the other speculations are entirely beside the point.

49. What does our creed mean when it says that "Jesus descended into Hell"? Did Jesus actually go to Hell?

The Bible nowhere says that "He descended into Hell," but rather "into Hades," the place of the dead. Here He went to proclaim a finished redemption, and when He arose He led all the redeemed souls from Hades ("sheol" in the Old Testament) into Heaven. David prophesied of Jesus:

Thou wilt not leave my soul in hell [sheol] Ps. 16:10.

50. Please explain to me why Jesus said on the Cross, "My God, my God, why hast thou forsaken me?" Did He feel that way? He knew He was giving His life to save humanity, and as a martyr He should have felt differently.

Concerning the cry of our Lord on the Cross, "My God, my God, why hast Thou forsaken Me?" this, of course, refers to the fact that He was there paying for the sins of the world; and since God could not look upon sin, He forsook Him, and Jesus experienced the agonies of being separated from God, which means, of course, the tortures of Hell, in order that we might be saved. He was forsaken of God in order that we might not be forsaken.

51. Someone told me that Jesus was colored. I wonder if there is any Scripture to prove this.

The Bible is very clear that Jesus was of the seed of Abraham, and the lineage of David. This, of course, would make Him a Jew, and not a colored man. Since Mary was a direct descendant of David, and Jesus had no human blood, this would make Him in His humanity a Jew. Of course, we know that He was also Deity, but as to His humanity, there is no question about the nationality. He was a Jew.

52. Where in the Bible will I find the statement I heard you make that there is in Heaven today a man, a human being with human body of flesh and bone bearing nail prints in his hands and feet, and yet at the same time very God of very God?

If you will turn to I Timothy 2, verse 5, you will find mention made of the Man Christ Jesus, who is now in Heaven as the Mediator between God and man.

Our Lord Jesus ascended in His resurrection body; and since this resurrection body was the human body of the Lord Jesus resurrected from the grave and consisting of flesh and bone, He ascended into Heaven in that same form, and is there today as a Man of flesh and bone, and with the print of the nails in His hands. In Luke 24:39 you will find the reference to His hands and His feet, and flesh and bones:

> Behold my hands and my feet, that it is I myself: handle me, and see; for a spirit hath not flesh and bones, as ye see me have (Luke 24:39).

In Zechariah 13:6 we have the Lord Jesus presented at His Second Coming as having the wounds still in His hands:

> And one shall say unto him, What are these wounds in thine hands? Then he shall answer, Those with which I was wounded in the house of my friends (Zech. 13:6).

The Bible nowhere says that flesh and BONE cannot inherit the kingdom of God, but instead it says, "flesh and BLOOD cannot inherit the kingdom of God" (I Cor. 15:50).

53. I heard a speaker say that Jesus had a very serious illness during His life on earth which left Him disfigured. He took one of the psalms as his basis for this, and then quoted from Isaiah 53 concerning His disfigurement. Would you give me your opinion on this teaching.

Since I did not hear the statement made myself, it is rather difficult for me to pass judgment on it. However, I can tell you very frankly that I do not believe that the Lord Jesus was afflicted with any loathsome or horrible disease. I imagine that probably the speaker was referring to Psalm 38, verse 7:

> For my loins are filled with a loathsome disease: and there is no soundness in my flesh.

But if we read this Psalm carefully, we will notice that David is speaking NOT about the Lord Jesus Christ, but ABOUT HIMSELF. The fact that our Lord bore our sicknesses and carried our diseases was fulfilled according to Matthew 8:17 when He went about on earth healing the sick and the afflicted.

> That it might be fulfilled which was spoken by Esaias the prophet, saying, Himself took our infirmities, and bare our sicknesses (Matt. 8:17).

I personally believe that the Lord Jesus Christ had no sin whatsoever in Him; and while He assumed our humanity, certainly He did not assume our sinful nature; and I personally feel that there is no Scriptural foundation for thinking that He carried in His blood a loathsome disease.

54. Will we see God the Father and God the Spirit separately from God the Son when we get to Heaven?

We will not be able to see God the Father and God the Spirit in Heaven, but we will see all of them in the Person of the Lord Jesus Christ only. Jesus said while He was here on earth:

> . . . he that hath seen me hath seen the Father (John 14:9).

55. In telling of the crucifixion of Jesus, why does Matthew record it, "They gave Him VINEGAR to drink mingled with GALL," and in the Book of Mark it states they offered Him "WINE mingled with MYRRH."

> They gave him VINEGAR to drink mingled with GALL: and when he had tasted thereof, he would not drink (Matt. 27:34).
> And they gave him to drink WINE mingled with MYRRH: but he received it not (Mark 15:23).

There is a difference of opinion with regard to this among theologians. Some believe that it was two different acts — that they gave Him both the vinegar and gall, and also the wine mingled with myrrh. It is usually supposed that the Lord refused to take the wine and the myrrh (Mark 15:23) because He did not want His sensibilities dulled in any way, but wanted to suffer all the agony, fully conscious of what was going on. It would appear that these do not refer to the same incident, but were

two separate incidents, for Jesus did take of the vinegar
offered Him (John 19:30).

56. If the Old Testament prohibited leaving the house on the Sabbath, how do you account for Jesus' observance of the Sabbath in the Synagogue?

In the Bible observance of the Sabbath, we must remember that when the Sabbath was originally given to
Israel, there was only one place of worship permitted,
which of course, was at Jerusalem in the Temple. During
those silent years between the close of Malachi and the
coming of the Lord Jesus Christ, the synagogue had
sprung up, and instead of one central place of worship
in Jerusalem, there were synagogues scattered and located
all through the Land of Israel. This, of course, was not
according to the Lord's commandment, for there is not
a single verse in the Bible which commanded them to
do so.

When the Lord, however, came into the world unto
His own, He found this condition, and in order to reach
His fellow Jews, He must of necessity find them together
in the synagogue. Just where the privilege of leaving
the house on the Sabbath day began and on what authority we do not know, but it does seem that at some subsequent time to the giving of the law and the prohibition
in the Book of Exodus concerning leaving their dwelling
places, they were permitted to make limited journeys
on the Sabbath day. It is not stated that there was any
authority for doing so, and it, of course, raises the question, as you put it, whether the Jews themselves were
not breaking the Sabbath by their synagogue worship.
Certainly the Lord had very little good to say for the
way the legal incrustations of the Sabbath had taken away

the real meaning of the day. Of course, we must always remember that Jesus was Lord of the Sabbath, and while He kept the law of God perfectly in every detail and fulfilled it completely by His death on the Cross of Calvary, He Himself was the Author and the originator of that law. There are, of course, some questions which are not entirely clear, but they are nothing compared with the confusion which results when we accept the Seventh-day Adventist's position.

57. Who crucified Christ?

To answer this question we must refer to several Scriptures. First, God GAVE His Son:

> For God so loved the world, that he gave his only begotten Son, that whosoever believeth in him should not perish, but have everlasting life (John 3:16).

Then Jesus GAVE HIMSELF:

> I am crucified with Christ: nevertheless I live; yet not I, but Christ liveth in me: and the life which I now live in the flesh I live by the faith of the Son of God, who loved me, and GAVE HIMSELF for me (Gal. 2:20).

The soldiers crucified Him:

> Then the soldiers of the governor took Jesus into the common hall, and gathered unto him the whole band of soldiers (Matt. 27:27).

The Jews murdered Him:

> Him, being delivered by the determinate counsel and foreknowledge of God, ye have taken, and by wicked hands have crucified and slain (Acts 2:23).

In a sense the Jews killed Christ. Actually the Roman soldiers did the crucifying. But spiritually, we all were the murderers. Basically, no one killed Christ, for Jesus laid down His own life, for He said:

> No man taketh it from me, but I lay it down of myself (John 10:18).

For ourselves, we must admit, OUR SINS KILLED HIM:

> All we like sheep have gone astray; we have turned every one to his own way; and the Lord hath laid on him the iniquity of us all (Isa. 53:6).

God gave His Son, sinners crucified Him, but Jesus died a voluntary death!

58. Did Jesus ever go into the Temple to pray?

I do not know that there is any Scripture which definitely says that Christ went into the Temple to pray. He did go into the Temple in order to rebuke the Pharisees, and also to cleanse the Temple; but I do not find any evidence that while He was there He prayed. He accused the priests of changing the Temple from a house of prayer into a den of thieves. This may account for His not praying in the Temple.

59. My son-in-law and I have had a disagreement as to how many were present at the ascension of Christ into Heaven. He says there were 500 present. Can you help us on this matter?

Your son-in-law is confusing the ascension into Heaven and the appearance of Christ to five hundred. I believe that he probably confuses the record of the ascension in Acts, chapter 1, with the appearance of the Lord Jesus Christ after His resurrection as recounted in I Corinthians, chapter 15. We believe that the Lord did appear unto five hundred people at one time, between His resurrection and His ascension, but also that on the day of His ascension only the eleven disciples were present to behold His going away. There is no mention of the five hundred in the first chapter of the Book of Acts. See Acts 1:1-9.

60. Where in the Bible does it state the season of the year when Christ was born?

There is nothing in the Bible whatsoever that gives us the season or the date or the month of the year in which Christ was born. The Lord evidently did not want us to remember His birthday, and so He has left it a matter which is not revealed. This is also true regarding His resurrection. However, we are absolutely sure that He arose on the first day of the week, as given in the account in Matthew and Luke, and is remembered and celebrated from the time of the early Christians until now.

61. Was the opening of the graves at the time of the crucifixion, or at the time that Christ arose?

In regard to the people in Matthew 27 who came out of their graves on the resurrection day, I believe that these constitute the "firstfruits" of the first resurrection. The graves were opened on the day of His crucifixion, but they did not arise from the grave until after the resurrection of Christ, and I firmly believe that they ascended with Him into Heaven and are there today in resurrection bodies as the earnest and the promise of our coming resurrection. The wording of Matthew 27:51-53 indicates that these saints arose AFTER JESUS AROSE.

> And, behold, the veil of the temple was rent in twain from the top to the bottom; and the earth did quake, and the rocks rent;
>
> And the graves were opened; and many bodies of the saints which slept arose,
>
> And came out of the graves AFTER HIS RESURRECTION, and went into the holy city, and appeared unto many (Matt. 27:51-53).

Chapter V

CHURCH ORDINANCES

62. I was told that infant baptism takes the place of circumcision, but I cannot seem to find the Scripture to back this statement.

The reason you have been unable to find the Scripture to back this statement is because the Bible does not contain anything whatsoever concerning this subject. There is no record in the Bible where babies were ever baptized, much less sprinkled. There is only one form of baptism taught in the Bible, and that is by immersion, and this is only for believers. We believe that the covenant God made with Abraham in Genesis 17:7, had to do with the literal, physical seed of Abraham, and the Land of Canaan.

> And I will establish my covenant between me and thee and thy seed after thee in their generations for an everlasting covenant, to be a God unto thee, and to thy seed after thee.

That this verse refers to the literal, physical seed is made perfectly clear by the next verse in which God continues to say:

> And I will give unto thee, and to thy seed after thee, the LAND wherein thou art a stranger, all the LAND OF CANAAN, for an everlasting possession; and I will be their God (Gen. 17:8).

From this it is quite evident that the Abrahamic covenant as used in Genesis 17 is a covenant for the Nation of Israel with Abraham's physical seed in regard to the Land of Canaan.

God promises in His Word that if we will "train up a child in the way that he should go, when he is old he will not depart from it" (Prov. 22:6). We have a right to claim God's promises for our children, but they certainly are not saved because they are born of Christian parents, or because they have been sprinkled as babies, nor are they covenant children; but they must come to a personal knowledge and acceptance of the Lord Jesus Christ as their own personal Saviour.

63. Is there a difference between John's baptism and the Christian baptism of today, or are they both the same?

In regard to John's baptism and the Christian baptism, Acts 19 is sufficient to show the fact that they are NOT the same. The baptism of John was the "kingdom" baptism associated with the offer of the Kingdom message to Israel by Jesus and His disciples. It is the same baptism as the baptism administered by the disciples at Pentecost. If you will read carefully the 10th chapter of Matthew, you will see that the commission was strictly apostolic, and to Israel only, and had no reference to the Gentiles whatsoever, and of course, the Church is not in view.

After the offer of the Kingdom had been finally rejected by the Nation of Israel, climaxing in the stoning of Stephen, Christian baptism comes in view, which is a testimony of our faith in the Lord Jesus Christ, and not a condition of salvation. This is the only view which can explain why the disciples in Ephesus were RE-baptized (Acts 19:1-5).

64. What does the water and blood signify which came from Christ's body when they thrust the spear into His side? There is a group who say it signifies baptism as being essential to salvation as well as the blood.

Concerning the water which came from the side of the Lord Jesus Christ when the spear point was thrust into His side, we must remember that it was not only water, but it was also blood. The Bible says that "there came out blood and water" (John 19:34). This has absolutely nothing to do with baptism. It was the proof of Jesus' death. It is a scientifically established fact that when people die, the blood in the heart separates into its fluid and solid constituents. The fluid is called the serum or the plasma, and the solid part is composed of the corpuscles. The water spoken of in the Bible was this serum which came from our Lord's side, and was the proof that He had actually and really died. There is nothing here to substantiate the statement that baptism is essential to salvation.

65. Should a pastor refuse baptism to a candidate who does not join his church?

One cannot judge the refusal of a pastor to baptize a person because he does not join the church. It is hard to give a definite answer because it depends upon the local regulations. If it is the rule of the church not to baptize anyone unless they join the church, then, of course, the pastor must abide by that rule, or be found unfaithful to his promise to the group he serves.

Personally, I do not believe that it is necessary to join a church to be baptized; but since I am not the pastor of the church, it is impossible for me to say what they ought to do. Personally, I would baptize anybody upon confession of their faith in the Lord Jesus Christ; but those who are pastors of churches must abide by the regulations of the church and the denomination, or else step out.

66. Is speaking in tongues a sign of faith?

Apostolic speaking in tongues was a temporary gift. We believe that this was a dispensational sign for the apostolic age only, before the New Testament was completed and all the books of the Bible had been given to us. We do not believe that the Lord today wants us to depend upon signs, but to simply believe His word. Tongues are not an evidence of great faith, but according to Scripture tongues and signs are an evidence of weak faith. It was given to babes in Christ, during the infancy of the Church. We believe that it was particularly for the Jewish nation, and that with the completion of the Bible, they have ceased. I am sure that if you continue studying the Word, that these things will become clear to you. Read carefully I Corinthians 13:11,

> When I was a child, I spake as a child, I understood as a child, I thought as a child: but when I became a man, I put away childish things (I Cor. 13:11).

67. In our family we have been faced with the following problem: Must children be baptized before being permitted to take of the communion?

In the Baptist Church of which you are a member, one requirement is that they shall be baptized by immersion before they can become members, and before they can partake of communion. However, we do not believe that baptism is necessary for salvation, but that it is done in obedience to the example of the Lord. Therefore, if you are a member of the Baptist Church, then it is perfectly proper that the member should be baptized before being admitted to the communion table. If you feel that this position of the Baptists is wrong, then you should seek other fellowship, and not make trouble over your opinion.

68. I would like to be baptized by immersion. I have been a Methodist for many years and the Baptist church here hesitates to baptize me until I join their church. Should I just be content, then, not to be baptized?

The Bible nowhere teaches that it is necessary to join a particular church in order to be immersed. However, I do believe that it is in obedience to the example of Christ that one ought to be immersed as a testimony of their salvation; although when it is impossible because of physical disabilities, I believe that the Lord understands these things also. If you can find a good Baptist church where you can be in fellowship, you should be willing to conform to their custom and requirements. Fellowship is more important than our personal opinions on non-essentials.

69. I am the teacher of a Bible class, and through my ministry one of the pupils has accepted Christ, and now wants to be baptized. However, she would like to have me perform the baptism and I am not an ordained minister but a layman. In your opinion would I be qualified to perform a baptismal service?

There is no Biblical injunction which makes it mandatory for ordained ministers or special officers to perform the ordinance. As far as the Bible is concerned, baptism can be performed by any born-again true believer. However, it is the custom in the churches, that it be limited to those who are in an official position, especially pastors and preachers; and this of course throws a different light on it. It is not a matter of your "right" to baptize, but a matter of the expediency of doing so. Paul says, "All things are lawful for me, but all things are not expedient: all things are lawful for me, but all things edify not" (I Cor. 10:23). Therefore, if you were to antagonize the other Christians, and the church, by performing a baptism which they would frown upon, you might be injuring your testimony even though you might not be doing anything contrary to the Word of God. For this reason I feel that if there is any objection in your local community to your performing this baptism, that it would be better to have it done in accordance with the usage in the community and the church.

I hope that you understand my position. Personally I have absolutely no objection to anyone baptizing another, if they are both born again. However, we are in the world, and we must bear testimony for Christ; and if we become a stumbling-block to weaker Christians, it is probably better if we just accommodate ourselves to the conditions rather than creating a division among the people of God.

70. **Some friends of mine were baptized in their own church. They have now moved into our community and would like to join our church. However, our pastor says they must be baptized again. They feel that they would be denying their first baptism if they had it done over. Please let me know your opinion in this matter.**

I cannot see any reason at all why these friends of yours from the other church should not be received into your membership without the necessity of being re-baptized. I personally do not feel that if anyone has been baptized in good faith, that it ever needs to be repeated. After all, it doesn't make any difference who does the baptizing, as long as it is an expression on the part of those baptized, of their faith in the blood of the Lord Jesus Christ. Certainly I would not insist upon a re-baptism in a case of this kind. In fact, I think it wrong to submit to being baptized again just to please some sectarian, bigoted group.

Of course, I realize that this is only my personal opinion, and if it is a rule of your church that they must be re-baptized, there is little that you can do about it. When one belongs to a church, of course, one should submit himself to its rules and regulations insofar as it is not in contradiction to the Word of God, or else resign quietly and go where you can agree.

71. **In organizing an independent Baptist church the question has arisen as to whether we should accept triune immersion (three times forward). Is there any definite Scripture to prove which is the proper mode and why either one should not be accepted? Also should those seeking membership who have been baptized before, be re-baptized for membership with us?**

Concerning the organization of your church and the method of baptism to be followed, I believe that we can make so much of the METHOD that we lose the MESSAGE of baptism entirely. Personally, I feel that the usual custom of baptizing people by immersion, once backward, is all which is required. After all, we do not bury people with their face downward, but on their back. Baptism is compared to burial (Romans 6). While there may not be a valid argument for this method, I believe that we should not cause any division among the believers by insisting upon other methods, as long as the Bible does not explicitly state just exactly in what order it is to be done. I regret deeply this dissension among believers who insist upon being baptized three times, or forward, or backward, or any other method, and thus obscure the spiritual significance of the ordinance.

Concerning the matter of re-baptism of those who have already been baptized before, I do not believe that it is necessary. I do not believe that the baptism depends upon the particular organization or individual who performs it, but upon the personal faith of the one who is baptized. Of course, there is no absolute statement in the Bible as to the exact mode in which it should be done, and so I believe that we ought to be very charitable in regard to these differences of opinion.

72. I understand that you do not believe in "closed communion." What is your reason?

My reason for holding the position against a closed communion of any denomination is simply that there is only One True Church. Denominationalism was utterly unknown in the early apostolic church, and we find nothing of it in the Book of Acts. We do find the seeds of sectarianism and denominationalism in the writings to the Corinthians, but it is severely condemned by the Apostle Paul. We therefore believe in the oneness of the Body of the Lord Jesus Christ, and that all those who are members of that Body and are not living in unconfessed sin, are welcome to the Table of the Lord, and it is open to all those who are walking in fellowship with Him.

73. Are the Passover Supper and the Lord's Supper two different events? I had never thought that the supper

was different from Jesus taking the cup and the bread. Am I right?

According to the Word of God, the Lord's Supper was first observed in the upper room by Jesus and the disciples, but not until AFTER the celebration of the Passover and the institution of the foot-washing. We believe the order to have been as follows: first, the passover feast for the last time, at which Judas was still present; then followed the foot-washing during which time Judas evidently left the upper chamber; and then after that, the Lord instituted the Lord's Supper with His disciples. I think that this is in perfect harmony with all of the four Gospel records. The Lord's Supper is NOT a continuation of the Passover, but a NEW ORDINANCE for the Church in this dispensation.

CHAPTER VI

CULTS, ISMS, AND RELIGIONS

74. What is the social gospel?

The social gospel is a modernistic gospel which in general denies the Deity of Christ, and the need for a blood atonement. It teaches that by the preaching of a so-called gospel for society and better understanding and culture, the world will gradually become better and better, until all men will live at peace among each other. It preaches a Kingdom without the return of the King. It ignores the redemptive purpose for eternity, and, in general, does not teach future punishment and retribution.

It is a counterfeit gospel which ought to be avoided, and while it is gaining ground in many denominational circles today, we still believe that—

> This is a faithful saying, and worthy of all acceptation, that Christ Jesus came into the world to save sinners (I Tim. 1:15).

75. What are the Seventh-Day Baptists, and are they the same as the Adventists?

There is such a group, although it is very small, and I am personally not too familiar with them. I know of one Seventh-day Baptist Church here in Michigan, but do not know too much about their doctrines and beliefs.

51

They are, however, not Seventh-day Adventists, but seem to be Baptistic in most of their doctrine, while holding to the seventh day as the Sabbath, rather than the first day of the week as the Lord's Day.

I do not believe that they have any direct connection with the Miller movement of the early nineteenth century. Of course, we believe that the Seventh-day AD-VENTISTS are absolutely unscriptural by putting people back under the law, and denying the grace of God. I do not believe that this is true of the Seventh-day Baptist Church.

76. When did the Seventh-day Adventist church start?

The Seventh-day Adventist religion really began as far back as 1840 A. D., but was made official after the prophecies and testimonies of Mrs. Ellen White concerning the Second Coming of Christ in 1843. The movement originated with the setting of a definite date for Christ's return. When the Lord did not come back in 1843, they set another date, and this too was not fulfilled. From then on, they have been floundering around, trying to set dates, and mixing up law and the Gospel, until they are the most confused sect in the world today. There is probably not a more evil, deceptive cult.*

77. I am in possession of some literature put out by the Review and Herald Publishing Association. Can you tell me if this is all right to pass on, and who publishes this material?

The Review and Herald Publishing Association is the name of the Seventh-day Adventist Publishing House,

---

*For more information write to the Radio Bible Class, Grand Rapids, Michigan, and ask for the booklet by Dr. M. R. De Haan, "What Do Seventh-day Adventists Believe Today?"

and is, of course, greatly in error, and it is dangerous literature. They dress it up with the Gospel, but underneath they come with their religion of works, and all the other errors for which they are known. They do not come out directly, but get people to take their publications, and then bit by bit begin to feed them the poison of their erroneous doctrine. The very fact that they do not tell you who they are, proves that the whole thing is deception. I am sorry that you were fooled by them, but I am sure that you will not succumb to them again.

78. I have heard of the ministry of Dr. Albert Schweitzer and his missionary endeavors, and was wondering if he is really a fundamental Gospel worker or not.

From my understanding and investigation, Dr. Albert Schweitzer is more of a social worker and preacher of a social gospel than a fundamental missionary. I am of the opinion and impression from all that I have read about him, that he is definitely a modernist, and does not place proper value upon the blood, but more upon human works, reformation, and social uplift. This is as far as my knowledge of him goes, but from all of my research, I find nothing that would credit him as a fundamentalist in any sense of the word.

79. Where does the Roman Catholic Church get its teaching of "the sinlessness of the Immaculate Virgin Mary, the Mother of Jesus"?

This doctrine was made a tenet of the Roman Catholic Church many centuries after the Bible was written, and simply affirmed that Mary was born without sin, and therefore Jesus had no sin. It of course answers nothing, for it only pushes the question back one generation. The

authority for this doctrine is the Roman Church — NOT
THE BIBLE.

**80. What did Jesus mean when He said to Peter, "On this
rock I will build My Church." A Catholic friend tells
me that Peter is the rock. I am unable to answer her.**

Jesus is the Rock. In the verse in Matthew 16:18,
Jesus says:

> . . . thou art Peter, and upon this rock I will build my
> church (Matt. 16:18).

The word translated "Peter" in the Greek is "petros"
(a little stone), and the word for "rock" is "petra" (Greek
word for "rock"). Jesus is the Rock, and Peter is one
of the stones in the building of the Church. Peter understood it this way, and was the very last person to claim
he was the Rock (read what Peter himself says in I Peter
2:4-8).

> To whom coming, as unto a living stone, disallowed
> indeed of men, but chosen of God, and precious,
> Ye also, as lively stones, are built up a spiritual house, an
> holy priesthood, to offer up spiritual sacrifices, acceptable
> to God by Jesus Christ.
> Wherefore also it is contained in the scripture, Behold,
> I lay in Sion a chief corner stone, elect, precious: and he
> that believeth on him shall not be confounded.
> Unto you therefore which believe he is precious: but unto
> them which be disobedient, the stone which the builders
> disallowed, the same is made the head of the corner,
> And a stone of stumbling, and a rock of offence, even to
> them which stumble at the word, being disobedient: where-
> unto also they were appointed (I Peter 2:4-8).

**81. Did Mary remain a virgin after Jesus was born? Some-
one told me she did.**

The Catholic Church teaches as follows:

> "In 649, the Lateran Council under Pope Martin I de-

fined that Mary was a virgin, not only before and after, but also during the birth of Christ. The obvious meaning of this, according to every Catholic theologian is that at the appointed time, Our Blessed Lord left the womb of His Mother through the natural channels but in a miraculous way, that is, without in any manner opening any part of Mary's body. In other words, there was no dilation of the normal passage, no opening of the vagina, no breaking of the virginal hymen. The body of the Saviour passed through Mary's body into the outside world much as the light goes through the glass without in any way damaging its integrity . . . the truth of Christ's miraculous birth, as explained above very concisely, rests chiefly on the infallible authority of the Magisterium. For a Catholic, that ends the argument 'without further explanations' being necessary."

(Taken from "The Sunday Visitor,"
April 14, 1957).

This, of course, has no foundation at all in Scripture, for the Bible plainly states that Mary had other children. Jesus had brothers and sisters.

Is not this the carpenter's son? is not his mother called Mary? and his brethren, James, and Joses, and Simon, and Judas?

And his sisters, are they not all with us? Whence then hath this man all these things? (Matt. 13:55, 56).

Is not this the carpenter, the son of Mary, the brother of James, and Joses, and of Juda, and Simon? and are not his sisters here with us? And they were offended at him (Mark 6:3).

82. I have heard of a group who claim the power of healing and other miracles, and as a sign of their power say that oil drips from their hands. Can you tell me how oil can drip from their hands?

I have met some of these folks who claim that oil drips from their hands, and the only evidence that I have been able to detect is that they were sweating in the palms of their hands, due to an overwrought, nervous condition. I do not believe that there is any truth whatsoever in the claims which are made by these poor, deluded souls. Certainly there is nothing in the Word of God that gives them any encouragement at all for making the claims they do. I do not doubt that among them there are sincere Bible-believing Christians, but they certainly have not been taught, and do not know the true meaning of the work of the Holy Spirit. If I were you, I would pay no attention to them whatsoever, but seek to get them under sound Bible teaching, and straightened out in their many errors.

I am certain that it is not of the Lord, and that it is due entirely to an emotional upset and a misunderstanding of the Word of God. Let us pray for these poor, deluded souls, that they may find the peace that comes by trusting Christ alone, without asking for additional signs and wonders.

83. Could you tell me anything about a group which call themselves "Friends" or "Quakers"?

They are a religious group which dates back several hundred years, and were so called because they shook and quaked during their services. It was at first a sort of nickname, but today it is accepted as identifying a certain group of people who believe in silent meetings, and do not practice the ordinances, and do not usually have stated pastors. Some of the Friends churches are quite fundamental while others are not. It all depends upon the leaders which they have. The characteristic things about the Friends or the Quakers are that they are definitely opposed to war of any kind, and are conscientious objectors.

84. I have received some literature in the mail from the "Moral Re-Armament organization." Can you tell me anything about this group? Are they worthy of support?

I am not sufficiently acquainted with the organization, which seems to be of Canadian origin, to give you any definite advice as to its worthwhileness. I have come in contact with some of its publications from time to time, and it appears that they are a patriotic organization which is seeking by political and educational means to solve the problems of the world. As such I believe that they are sincere and earnest and honest in their efforts, but beyond this I know practically nothing about them.

Personally, of course, we believe that the only answer to the world's problems is the Gospel of the Lord Jesus Christ, and not human wisdom or understanding. While men may be very sincere in their efforts to bring about peace and happiness, we must realize that it can never come, apart from the Lord Jesus Christ. Personally, therefore, I believe that one can much better give his support to the Gospel than to these movements, even though they may have some civic merit.

Chapter VII

CHURCHES AND DENOMINATIONS
(*Discipline* & *Doctrine*)

85. Do you believe that a born-again Christian should belong to a local church if it is true to the Lord and preaching the Gospel, and if so, why?

Concerning your question, I would like to refer you to Hebrews 10:25,

> Not forsaking the assembling of ourselves together, as the manner of some is; but exhorting one another: and so much the more, as ye see the day approaching (Heb. 10:25).

This should answer your question in regard to the advisability of belonging to a local church. I believe it is the duty of every believer to associate himself with other believers for the purpose of worshiping and assembling together in preparation for the work of the Lord.

86. Do you feel that visual aids have a place in teaching the Word?

I have nothing against the proper use of visual aids and pictures in order to help get the message out. However, I am concerned over the present trend toward an extreme position in this matter, to the minimizing or neglect of "preaching" the Word, which after all is the important thing in every service. Where pictures are shown and accompanied by the plan of salvation being clearly preached, we should have no objection. It can be a great aid in illustrating the Word of God. However, I am deeply concerned at the trend which things are taking today, where many services are becoming more of an entertainment than Bible preaching.

87. Do you think we are justified in leaving a church of which we have been a member, because it has gone modernistic?

I am sorry that I am not in a position to give you any concrete advice, since I do not know all of the facts. I am not familiar with the situation in your community, and what the pastor of the church stands for. All I can say is that if a church does not preach the pure Gospel of the grace of God, and has drifted away from the purpose for which a church is organized; namely, to preach only Christ and Him crucified, then it becomes one's duty to leave such an organization and go with those who are faithful to the trust of preaching the whole Gospel of Christ to a lost world. If this is the situation, then you will have to trust the Lord in making the move as He leads you. I hope that you will understand that it is quite difficult to pass judgment on a situation where one does not know all of the details. However, I do know that there are many churches today that are not preaching the full Gospel, and if I belonged to one of these, I certainly would get out as quickly as possible.

88. The nearest church to our home is the "Church of Christ." Do you think it is all right for us and our family to attend there?

I do not agree with some of the teachings of this denomination. They do not believe in the pre-millennial coming of the Lord Jesus Christ, and they place so much emphasis on water baptism that it is made a requisite for salvation.

However, if there is no other place to fellowship, then you are almost compelled to attend there, but you must exercise your own gift of discernment in taking what is Scriptural, and rejecting that which is against the Word of God. If there is a sound Baptist church within reasonable distance, I certainly would advise you to go there, rather than to the Church of Christ.

89. Do you think it is important to belong to a denomination?

You must remember that there are absolutely no denominations mentioned in the Bible. These all came since the Book of Acts, and we do not believe that membership in a denomination is the important thing at all, but rather membership in the Body of Christ.

90. I attend a Methodist church where candles are lit on the altar, and I do not feel that this is Scriptural. Can you help me?

There are practices in some of the worldly churches which cause us to be greatly alarmed. So many empty religious forms are practiced in churches today. Certainly there is nothing in the Bible at all which gives us any occasion for using all the "trappings" which are found in some churches, including their altar and candle lighting, and many other pagan practices. I believe that the entire candle service is just a remnant of paganism passed on to us through the Roman Catholic Church and certainly has no place whatsoever in a truly fundamental, spiritual church. It is a sad thing that the Methodist Church, which years ago was such a power for God, has degenerated to where there are very, very few men left in it who really know what the Gospel is all about. We ought to pray for them, that the Lord may convict them, and lead His dear people out.

91. What do you think of the World Council of Churches?

We cannot commend the World Council of Churches, and cannot be too emphatic in warning against it. It is a cage of "clean and unclean birds and beasts" together, and in the main is composed of modernists who deny all the cardinal doctrines of the Word of God which are so precious to us. I do not believe that a truly born-again believer has any right to belong to this organization. I have always warned other preachers against it, although there are in it many God-fearing men who should know better.

92. Can you tell me just when the Catholic Church was organized? I have heard some say this was the first church, but I thought Israel was, as long as she was in the wilderness.

As to the exact date of the organization of the Roman Catholic Church, it is impossible to give this. As the Church of the Book of Acts progressed and grew, the corruptions of the Catholic Church soon crept in, and God called out the Protestant Churches during the Reformation as a protest against the corruption of the Catholic Church.

Neither the Catholic Church nor the Protestant Church is the TRUE CHURCH of Jesus Christ, but only those who constitute His Body. There were undoubtedly many, many thousands of born-again believers in the early Catholic Church, and we believe there are some in the Catholic Church today, but not all of the members of the Protestant churches are members of the Body of Christ either.

The Church is not the continuation of the Nation of Israel in any sense whatsoever. The two are totally distinct. God's promise to Israel will still be fulfilled when they will be completely regathered in the Land, while the Church will be caught up to meet the Lord in the air at the Rapture. There is only One True Church, and it consists of all born-again believers regardless of denomination or sect or nationality. What we call churches are local assemblies, but the One True Church is composed of all people who have trusted the finished work of the Lord Jesus Christ. This Church began at the day of Pentecost, and has never been interrupted.

93. We have a real problem in our church. Do you think it is right for the young people to sponsor dances in the church building?

Dances in the church building are of the Devil. I do not believe that the House of God is a place for these things at all; and while I am opposed to dances in general, I am still more opposed to having them in the church parlors.

94. Our church is having an Easter sunrise service with a breakfast to follow, and I do not know just what attitude to take on this situation. Please help me.

In regard to sunrise services for Easter, I feel that they can be used of the Lord, and I do not know that I would be too strongly opposed to the custom of having a breakfast. I have never seen the need of it, personally, and still do not; but these are matters which have to be settled on the basis of local conditions. Of course, you realize that there is absolutely no Scriptural basis for the celebration of Easter as it is observed today.

95. Is there a definite Scriptural pattern to follow in the church worship service?

There is no place in Scripture where a definite pattern or order of worship is laid down for Christians in this dispensation. The Holy Spirit should be given full sway, so that He may order the worship according to His own will. For the sake of orderliness and decency, it may be well to have some kind of fixed order, especially in large congregations, but there is nothing in the Bible which prescribes a certain order of worship. The Lord Jesus Christ said in John 4:24,

> God is a spirit: and they that worship him must worship him in spirit and in truth (John 4:24).

96. My wife and I attend a church which has gone very modernistic. We both have classes and teach these young people the way of salvation. While our membership is in this church, we do not agree with all of its program, and there is a smaller fundamental work which needs our help. We want to be in the will of the Lord, and need some advice as to just what move, if any, we should make. Can you help us?

I am sorry that I cannot give you a really definite answer, because it is one of those situations where one must be especially careful to make sure that he is being led of the Lord in whatever decision is made. However, I can give you my counsel and my advice, and then assure you that we shall be praying for you that the Lord may very definitely make His will known.

In regard to your present fellowship in the church, it is a very serious problem which you must not decide in a hurry. Sometimes it is best to remain in a church of this kind as long as you are able to have some influence; and especially in teaching a class, you may lead other precious souls to the Lord Jesus Christ. If you abandon the church entirely, of course, your contact is broken off.

On the other hand, your presence in a modernistic church of this kind might encourage other weak Christians to believe that you are endorsing the things that they are doing, and in this way you may have a bad influence on them. Whether to leave the church and to help some other struggling fundamental work, or whether to remain as long as you are being tolerated, is a real problem which no one can solve for you, but you yourself must decide.

However, I do believe that if you are faithful in your ministry there, the Lord Himself will lead you out. The important thing to remember is, not to run ahead of the Lord, but to let Him lead. I am sure that if you are faithful in your testimony, and do not in any way compromise, that the Lord Himself will thrust you out, rather than your having to take the initiative yourself.

Of course, I realize that it makes it very difficult for you to serve in a church where you are out of harmony with many things which they do, and if you find these things intolerable, of course, the only thing for you to do is to break your fellowship with them, and throw your lot in with others. I suppose that you have let the leaders of the church know what your stand and your convictions are, and as long as they tolerate you, I would wait for the Lord's definite leading before I made any step.

97. Our church is planning to show the "Martin Luther Film." What do you think of it?

I can recommend without reservation the Martin

Luther film. I have had the opportunity of seeing it myself, and find it a wonderful production, and there is absolutely nothing objectionable whatsoever. I feel that it would be a great service to your community and your church if they would have the opportunity of seeing this excellent production.

98. What do you think of having social functions and banquets in the church?

Concerning social functions, I believe that we must be careful to make a distinction between social functions which are sponsored by the church, and social functions which are indulged in by members of the church, without the sanction or supervision of the church.

I hold with you that the business of the church is to preach the Gospel, and not go into catering or banqueting or athletics; but, of course, we do not see any harm in individual members of the church getting together for a Christian, social gathering. I believe, therefore, that it ought to be kept separate from the church.

99. Do you think the Lord is pleased with the way some churches are carrying on their Vacation Bible School programs, having handcraft and leathercraft, and then while they are having their Bible lessons they do not have their minds on their work because they are thinking about the refreshments they will receive before they go home. Please give me your opinion on this.

It is quite impossible to state whether it is right or wrong, since I do not know all of the circumstances. However, I can say this, that the main purpose of Vacation Bible School is to teach the Word of God, and to give the children as much of the Bible as possible. I therefore feel that these other things are not essential, and belong to a secular school rather than a Vacation Bible School.

Please do not misunderstand me. I do not know just exactly what the conditions are, to which you refer; but for myself, I think that we ought to spend as much time of the short period that we have, in definite Bible study, rather than some of these other things. Of course, the leaders you have in mind may have other reasons and arguments for doing what they are doing, with which I am not familiar, and so I do not want to be too severe without knowing all the facts.

100. What do you think of hiring professional money raisers to finance a church building program?

Concerning hiring a professional organization in order to finance the work of the church, and to raise money, I do not know just exactly what the local situation is to which you refer, and so cannot pass judgment.

However, I can give you in a general way my own impression about this method of financing the Lord's work. I believe that it is usually a reflection upon the spirituality of the people if they must resort to these methods in order to keep God's business going. If the people are fully consecrated to the Lord and are of a willing mind, there should be enough to meet all the needs of the church. I have never been able to see the justification of taking a part of the money which is raised for the Lord's work and giving it to a commercial organization as a commission, especially if this organization is not composed of born-again Christians. I realize that this is quite popular today, but I do not feel that I personally could ever endorse such a method.

I believe that when we are faithful to the Lord He will

supply our need. The Radio Bible Class stands as a testimony to this truth; for in all the years that we have been on the air, we have never solicited money from the world, and we have never asked for anything over the air in any way, shape, or manner, and yet the Lord has always supplied our needs through His consecrated people.

I hope that you will understand that I am not passing judgment upon the individual situation to which you refer, as I do not know all the details, but I certainly do not feel that if people cannot give out of a willing heart, but have to be canvassed and pressure-ized, that they will receive any reward for their gifts. Let us pray much for one another that we may not be led astray by any of these modern methods.

101. My son belongs to a Lutheran Church where no person who has taken his own life can have a funeral service from the church. He would like to know your opinion concerning this matter.

The only way that we can answer the Lutheran position which you state, is to remind them that the Lord says that we are not to judge one another. I believe that we have to leave these things with the Lord, and we have no right either as an individual or a church, to pass upon the salvation of anyone who takes his own life. We do not know what the circumstances were, and we have to leave these things entirely in the hands of the Lord. I therefore do not agree with any church which would refuse a church funeral to those who had committed suicide.

102. We are faced with a problem concerning church discipline. A member of our church was married by

a Roman Catholic priest and signed any children over to the Catholic Church. He desires to remain in our church membership but cannot say he is sorry on these two counts because indirectly he feels it will mean he is sorry he married his wife. What Scriptural truth can be presented to clear up this matter?

From the facts you state, I certainly do feel that this man should admit his mistake in having signed over his children to the Roman Catholic Church, and for entering into an unequal yoke. The Bible is very clear that believers are not to be yoked with unbelievers, and I feel that you are quite right in asking him to publicly show his repentance and sorrow for this mistake. It is, of course, not a matter of asking him to leave his wife or anything of the kind. It is merely following the Scriptural principle that public sins must be publicly confessed.

I do not know whether there are other conditions and circumstances which might alter the picture, but from a purely Scriptural standpoint, it seems to me that the man should be willing to do this, and thus be maintained in fellowship, or be Scripturally disciplined for his error.

Chapter VIII

CHRISTIAN CONDUCT

103. The shop in which I am employed is joining the C.I.O. and those who do not sign in will lose their job. I do not feel that I can conscientiously join this group, and yet I cannot afford to lose my position. Do you think a Christian should belong to a labor union?

Concerning labor unions, we cannot legislate for others. I believe that this whole situation is one which is up to the individual, according to the Scripture, "Let every man be fully persuaded in his own mind" (Rom. 14:5). I do not feel that it is the right of anyone else to tell a man what to do and what not to do in a situation of this kind, though I have very definite convictions along this line, and am not ashamed to tell them.

Personally, I cannot endorse the labor union's methods, especially in the way they are being handled by the "higher ups." Many of them do not recognize God or Christ, and it is too often an atheistic association, all of its past tendencies having been away from God and away from Christ. I believe that it genders hatred among the classes, and certainly is a forerunner of the "Mark of the Beast" which we know will come after the Church has been taken out.

The Scripture that I use for myself is found in II Corinthians 6:14-17, which I think is very definite.

> Be ye not unequally yoked together with unbelievers: for what fellowship hath righteousness with unrighteousness? and what communion hath light with darkness?
>
> And what concord hath Christ with Belial? or what part hath he that believeth with an infidel?
>
> And what agreement hath the temple of God with idols? for ye are the temple of the living God; as God hath said, I will dwell in them, and walk in them; and I will be their God, and they shall be my people.
>
> Wherefore come out from among them, and be ye separate, saith the Lord, and touch not the unclean thing; and I will receive you (II Cor. 6:14-17).

If we are to line ourselves up with the things of the world, it is going to place us in a position where we shall not be able to be the witness we ought to be for the Lord Jesus Christ.

Please do not misunderstand me, because I am not trying to tell you what to do, but only giving you my own personal opinion. If I were faced with the same situation with which you are, I might look at it differently, but you will have to settle this with the Lord, and I am sure that if you will take a definite stand, the Lord Himself will honor you for such a stand.

104. Do you think it is all right for a Christian to use wine in moderation?

It is the ABUSE of wine, rather than the USE of wine which is strongly condemned in the Scriptures. I know that in European countries, even among Christians, wine is oftentimes used as an appetizer, but not to excess. Personally, I do not use it, and I wish that we could eliminate it entirely, but it is well to remember that the USE of wine does not mean the ABUSE of wine. Certainly it was never meant to be used for the purpose of intoxication, and I believe that it would be a great deal better not to use it at all, seeing the evil to which it often leads. There are only a few people who are able to do these things in moderation, and I find that the only sure cure for the awful evil of drinking is to leave it alone altogether. The advice that I give to people is: "If you never touch it, you will never abuse it."

105. It is my heart's desire to be in the will of the Lord. I have prayed much concerning what He would have me do, but thus far have had no definite leading. How can I know the Lord's will for me?

After asking God to show you His will for your life, and having received no definite answer, it is possible that the Lord still has to teach you some lessons before you are ready for His call. You must wait upon the Lord, and abide His own time. As long as you do not have any definite leading along any line, it is best to continue to serve faithfully where you are, and wait upon the Lord for His direction. Sometimes it takes a long, long time, but the Lord knows that we need the training of patience, and other things which cannot be learned in any other way. I would therefore just continue patiently in the place where you are, doing faithfully whatever lies at hand, and then in His own good time, when you are ready for the job, He will show you the path that you are to take.

I have experienced this in my own life. Sometimes we wondered why the answer to our prayers was delayed, but as we continued to wait upon Him, studying the Word, and believing His will to be best, sooner or later the answer came. We shall also be remembering you in prayer.

106. We have a new minister at our church, and he permits the deacons and other members who visit the parsonage to smoke there. Do you think this is right?

It is not up to me to tell the preacher what he can do in his own home, but I can only tell you what I personally feel in the matter. I do not believe that it is becoming for those who name the Name of Christ, and especially those who hold responsible positions to injure their testimony by this public offense. We all know that the use of tobacco is offensive to a great many people; and therefore these men, I believe, should be willing to give up what they consider to be a pleasure to them, for the sake of the testimony of Christ. This certainly would be the charitable and Christian thing to do.

I also feel that the preacher himself ought to recognize the fact that we are not to be an offense to others round about us who may be kept away from the Lord because of things that we do. Again, I cannot tell the preacher what he can do in his own home, but I can only tell you that in my opinion I think it very, very unwise to set up a barrier of offense by doing these things which belong to the world and certainly not to a consecrated Christian life.

Recent findings in the field of cancer research have definitely proven the use of tobacco is injurious to health. Since our bodies are God's temples, no one should damage the temple of God.

107. Should a Sunday night service be set aside for a banquet?

Sunday night is a wonderful time for a SPIRITUAL banquet, but setting aside a worship service for a social banquet is wrong. I do not believe that anything can take the place of the preaching of the Word. I certainly would not as a pastor of a church allow a banquet to be held on Sunday night, and give up the preaching service. I believe that the Lord's Day is for the specific purpose of preaching the Word, and nothing should be allowed to interfere.

108. I was told that if a Christian takes out fire insurance on his home, he is not trusting the Lord to take care of him. What do you think of this?

We have no right to judge one another in such matters. This again is a problem which must be settled between the individual and the Lord, or as the Bible puts it, "Let every man be fully persuaded in his own mind" (Rom. 14:5). Personally, I do not feel that it is a lack of faith and trust in the Lord, but only being "diligent in business" (Prov. 22:29). If a person feels that it is wrong to have his property insured, I suppose there is nothing that we can say against it, but I do believe that we have a right to make provision for emergencies which may arise. We do not object to the placing of money in the bank for a "rainy day," and carrying a reserve for emergencies. I believe that the Lord wants us to use our head in these things. There is a danger that we shall go off the deep end, and become fanatical in some of our views. As I said before, if anyone feels that it is wrong to carry fire insurance, I do not believe that they ought to do it; but I do not believe that we have a right to judge anyone who feels that it is all right to do so.

109. Is it right to have social security, or would this be classified in with gambling?

With this question again I believe that this is entirely a personal matter between yourself and the Lord. There is a great difference of opinion among Christians on this matter, just as there is on insurance and other situations. I do not believe that we are allowed to judge others, but they must follow their own conscience, and according to the Word of God "let every man be fully persuaded in his own mind."

Personally, I see no harm in utilizing the provision which is made by our government for our protection. After all, we use their police protection and fire protection and many other things, and I do not see where social security is any different. I hope this helps you in regard to your problem.

110. Should a Christian have gifts to the Lord receipted for income tax deductions?

Concerning the propriety of having your gifts recorded and receipted for income tax deductions, I personally feel that while we are not of the world, we are in the world, and we have to do some of these things for the sake of being subject to the powers that be. It is the law of the land that income tax be paid, and they have made it possible to make deductions for these charitable causes. Personally, therefore, I do not see anything wrong in keeping a record of contributions, and deducting the allowable portion. This will leave you more money to give to the Lord's work again. You might better give to God's work any money you can thus legally save.

111. A young man I know, felt he was definitely called to go into the ministry. He left his job and sold his home to go to school. Before he was able to get into the school his car broke down, and now he is back with his family in the city. He is a very spiritual young man,

and we cannot understand how, if he was so sure it was the Lord's will, that he was not able to go through with the plans. If it was not the Lord's will, how could he be so mistaken? I feel that no one can KNOW ABSOLUTELY when he is in the will of the Lord. Please help me in this problem.

The matter of knowing the will of God in regard to our lives is a matter which has been discussed by many, and there seems to be more or less difference and latitude of opinion. Personally, I feel that one's knowledge of the will of God in one's life is dependent very largely upon one's knowledge of the Word of God itself. The more we know the will of God as revealed in His Word, the easier it will be for us to determine just what He would have us to do.

The second thing which we must remember is that prayer is absolutely essential. The prayer of faith that believes that God will lead, must always be a part of our study of the Word of God.

Thirdly, we must exercise patience; and as long as we do not have a definite leading of the Lord, we should be willing to wait until we find absolute assurance in our own hearts that we are doing what His will is for our lives.

Then there is a fourth requisite which I think is overlooked by many. If God calls anyone to a certain task, they must also have the ability to perform that task. God does not call dumb people to speak, nor does He call blind people to read. If a person has no ability along a certain line, it is questionable whether God would call him to do anything which would be difficult for him. God does not expect us to do things which we are not able to do.

Of course, we cannot answer for anyone else, and each one of us must determine in what way the Lord reveals to us His precious will.

112. **My wife has received a questionnaire in regard to serving on a jury, and we know that Christ says in His Word that we should "judge not." In view of this, do you think a Christian should serve on a jury?**

Concerning your problem as to whether or not as a Christian you should serve on a jury, this question is more than one of judging—it is one of being obedient to the rulers of our land. Peter tells us in I Peter 2:13,

> Submit yourselves to every ordinance of man for the Lord's sake.

And in Romans 13:1 we read:

> Let every soul be subject unto the higher powers. For there is no power but of God: the powers that be are ordained of God.

The words of Jesus, "Judge not," refer rather to judgment upon insufficient evidence. However, everyone must be persuaded in his own mind. If you think it is wrong, don't do it. Of course, you cannot decide for your wife. She must do that herself.

113. **There is a possibility of selling our home to make way for a parking lot. We are in a commercial area and a landlord seeks to furnish parking facilities for his tenants. One of the stores in the block serves beer and there is also a liquor store whose customers would perhaps also make use of the parking space. Please advise us in this matter.**

I have read your letter very carefully, and trust that I can be of some help to you. Of course, it is not easy for us to put ourselves into your place, and to know just exactly what we would do in a case similar to this; but I do feel after careful consideration, that you are not responsible for what may happen to your property after you sell it. Since you are in a commercial block the time is not far off when it will be turned over for commercial purposes anyway, and I do not see that you have any responsibility as to what the purchaser may do with the property after you have sold it to him. I do not think that you can control the parking of those who may patronize a liquor store; and therefore, it is my honest opinion that if you sell your home, your responsibility ceases. Continue to pray definitely about it, and do as the Lord directs you.

114. **I was the innocent party in an accident and because of my injuries have a number of debts which I am unable to pay. According to the Word of God should I start suit to obtain money? Doesn't the Bible say that we should not go to law against one another?**

In view of the circumstances which you describe in your letter, I do not see any reason why you should not try to collect damages from the party who was to blame for your injury in your accident. The Bible prohibits "brother" going to law against "brother," in matters that can be taken care of in the assembly; but in matters of this kind, where it does not involve Christian fellowship, I believe that we have the right to use the provisions of the law which the Lord has established, and which are at our disposal.

115. **What do you think of Bible Story comics for Sunday School papers?**

Concerning the Sunday School literature which you enclosed, I certainly am not in favor of using this kind of material for teaching of our youngsters. It is copying the world, and I am afraid is only getting them used to the reading of other comics, and certainly cannot take the place of good, old-fashioned Bible teaching. However, I do not know what I can do about this to help you. You will have to work this out for yourself. If I were you, I would pray much for great wisdom that the Lord may help you to know just what to do in a situation of this kind. I certainly would not do anything hastily, but at least let your stand be known, and follow the Lord no matter what the cost may be.

116. What should be the Christian's attitude concerning capital punishment?

I have always believed that capital punishment antedated the law of Moses, and was laid down in the days of Noah (Gen. 9:5, 6), and is still binding today. I quite agree with you that Christians should have a different attitude toward capital punishment than the world has, because we are under grace. However, in speaking about capital punishment, we are looking at it from the legal aspect only, and the power of the constituted legal authorities to punish a man for a crime committed. Of course, I recognize the fact that under grace the Lord forgives. We too were under the sentence of capital punishment because of sin, but because of the blood of the Lord Jesus Christ we are freed from that punishment. However, in the world there is no such provision made, and the rule, "Whoso sheddeth man's blood, by man shall his blood be shed" (Gen. 9:6), still holds.

117. Do you think that pastors and churches should fight outwardly against such evils as bingo, pin ball, etc.?

The common practice of pastors and churches fighting evils such as bingo and other questionable amusements is, I believe, at best a negative approach. I believe that our approach should always be positive, showing men and women the better way of life through faith in the Lord Jesus Christ. Every time we get a sinner converted, the saloon and the theatre lose a customer. And if enough of them would be converted, of course, the places would have to shut down. I believe that this is the preacher's and the Christian's approach to these evils as we see them round about us today. As long as a man does not know the joy of serving the Lord Jesus Christ, we cannot blame him for seeking it in these other worldly pursuits. After all, it is the only thing he has; and I think that unless we can offer something better to take its place, that it is wrong to even try to take away what little fun he thinks he is having. I know that this idea is not the common opinion among a great many so-called "reformers," but I do believe that the positive preaching of the Gospel is the only antidote which we have for sin today.

118. In my work in a clinic I meet many people every day who are suffering pain, sorrow, heartache, and death. Can you advise me on the best way to be of help to these people?

This is a bigger problem than I can fully solve. For the proper approach to the sick, the dying, and the broken-hearted, there is no set formula, but each case must be dealt with on its own individual merits; and I believe that with much prayer and seeking of the Lord's will, we will be guided by the Spirit in giving exactly the right Scriptures and the right comfort to those who are in these unfortunate circumstances. Until the sufferer understands that this is part of God's wise plan, there can be little comfort.

119. **I have a real problem in my home concerning mixed bathing. My friend says we are doing more harm than good to our children by keeping them away from the pool, but I cannot go along with them as a Bible believer. Is swimming considered a worldly pleasure? Can you please help me in this?**

I can understand your problem very well, and also realize that it is difficult to live in this world and keep ourselves undefiled and unpolluted from it. Personally, I do not believe that there is any harm in swimming whatsoever. It is one of the innocent pleasures of life, and if it could be carried on under decent circumstances and conditions, there certainly could not be any objection to it. However, the evil lies in the attire which the swimmers wear. If proper clothing were worn at the beaches and the pools, I certainly would not want to condemn anyone for going in swimming. But it is the terrible lack of proper attire which is making it such an evil.

The best thing I can do for you, of course, is to pray for you that the Lord may give you wisdom in dealing with this difficult situation. As long as you are able to influence your girls in the right direction you must do so, but when it gets out of your control, then you must leave it with the Lord and make the best of a bad situation. I am sure that the Lord will give you wisdom in regard to this matter also.

120. Should a Christian vote in our country's elections?

I see nothing in the Scripture which would indicate that a Christian should not vote, but rather that it is his duty to do so; "the powers that be are ordained of God." (Read Romans 13:1-7.) We are to be subject to the higher powers. Jesus paid His taxes (see Matthew 22:21). We are to obey all the laws of the land as long as they do not conflict with the Word of God.

121. Is it wrong for a Christian to join the army or go to war?

This is a matter which must be decided by each one for himself. Our government recognizes the rights of "conscientious objectors" and makes provision for them in some other branch of service. However, it is my opinion that no citizen of any country at war can avoid going to war, even though not in the army. He pays taxes to carry on the war, he is engaged in producing the goods needed to carry on the war (foods, munitions, uniforms, etc.). It follows that everyone goes to war when the country does, whether at the front or at home.

In the Bible, soldiers were not expected to leave the army after they were saved (Matt. 8:5-13; Acts 10; Acts 27:43). We are not of the world, but we are still IN the world. Let every man be fully persuaded in his own mind.

122. Is it wrong for a woman to braid her hair? What does Peter mean by "plaiting" the hair in I Peter 3:3?

> Whose adorning let it not be that outward adorning of PLAITING THE HAIR, and of wearing of gold, or of putting on of apparel (I Peter 3:3).

Peter is not forbidding women to braid or plait their hair, but rather he is warning about the "extremes" of make-up and dress. This is evident from the rest of the verse where Peter says, "Whose adorning let it not be . . . adorning of plaiting the hair, or of wearing of gold, OR OF PUTTING ON OF APPAREL." If Peter condemns plaiting of the hair, he also condemns wearing clothes. This cannot be, of course, and so evidently Peter is thinking of putting undue emphasis on adorning the body. We should not live for these things. The temple of the Holy Spirit should be properly, attractively, but modestly, adorned.

123. I am concerned about our government preparing for the atomic war. Is it right for them to run all these atomic warfare tests as they are doing? Should we support such acts by the taxes we pay?

Concerning the government and these atomic weapons, I am sorry that we cannot be definite in our judgment regarding these matters. The government of the world is in the hands of the leaders of the nations, and is under the control of the Almighty; and while we may not agree with the things which are being done, we know that the "powers that be are ordained of God." It is therefore not our business to judge the government as to its national actions, but our main business is the preaching of the Gospel of the grace of God. The right and the wrong of these things will be judged by the Lord, but we must keep on doing nothing else but just preach the Word and be faithful. Of course, war is wrong, but we cannot stop it. Wars will continue to the end (Dan. 9:26), so let us be faithful to our one commission.

124. The other day some Christians had a party in honor of a couple's wedding anniversary and performed a "mock marriage." I did not attend as I felt it was

**mocking God. Please let me know what you think
of "mock marriages."**

Personally, I can see no harm in a mock wedding when
it is performed with due reverence, and as a reminder
of the vows which were spoken years before. It may
well serve to refresh in their memories the promises they
have made the one to the other. Of course, I do not
believe that it should be done in a frivolous or irreverent
way, but if it is done with emphasis on the solemnity
of the marriage relationship, I can see no harm in it. I
do not believe it comes under the definition of "mock-
ery." Of course, there are dangers of going to foolish
extremes, but I assume that this is not the case in your
situation.

125. **At a dinner meeting we had a guest minister who
spoke. He gave a fine talk and was well liked, but I
sat there and was uncomfortable because I knew that
he was in trouble in his church, and that his wife had
left him due to his actions. I sat quietly and made no
comment then or now. When men refer to him and
his talk what should my attitude be? Should I keep
quiet or discredit him as a minister?**

In Proverbs 17:9 we read:

> He that covereth a transgression seeketh love; but he that
> repeateth a matter separateth very friends.

Concerning your attitude toward the preacher who
has been living in sin, and is still carrying on his ministry,
I would advise that you do not take the responsibility
of exposing him. Undoubtedly there are some details
with which you are not familiar; and while we sincerely
regret that these things happen, we feel that it is best
not to publicize it before the world because of the stigma

it puts upon the Gospel of the Lord Jesus Christ. I believe it ought to be dealt with, of course, by the proper authorities of the church, but I personally do not feel that you ought to take the responsibility of starting the action. Then again, it is possible that he has sincerely repented and confessed his sins, and as such, we must be gracious and longsuffering with him. Remember, there are two sides to every matter. You may not know all the facts.

126. Do you believe it would or would not be sinful for me to work in a factory where rockets and satellites are manufactured? I would like to know your opinion, because I might have to make a decision in this regard in the future.

I know, and am persuaded by the Lord Jesus, that there is nothing unclean of itself: but to him that esteemeth any thing to be unclean, to him it is unclean (Rom. 14:14).

As to the advisability of taking employment in a factory where rockets and satellites are manufactured, I do not believe that it is possible for anyone to legislate in regard to what one Christian or another ought to do in regard to this matter. I think it is entirely between the individual and the Lord, and no one has a right to criticize whatever the decision may be. Personally, I do not see how we can be in this world without being directly or indirectly involved in some way with the program of destruction. Almost every line of industry and manufacture in some way or another is connected with the defense and armament effort, whether it be in the field of plastics or metals, or electrical devices or motors. Some way or another these find their way into airplanes and tanks and other instruments of destruction. I therefore do not see how any Christian can possibly avoid, while he is in this wicked world, having something to do with these matters.

My personal opinion, therefore, would be that if you feel led, and it is required of you that you should be employed in an occupation which may involve the manufacture of satellites and rockets, it is not for me nor anyone else to judge you in your decision. However, we can pray for one another that the Lord may lead and guide definitely in whatever decision must be made. I believe that in many of these matters the instructions of the Bible are applicable: "Let every man be fully persuaded in his own mind" (Rom. 14:5).

127. Should Christians tip waiters when served in restaurants?

This, of course, is a question which cannot be answered by either a "yes" or a "no." I believe that it is a matter which again is up to the individual. Personally, I feel that if the waiters and waitresses were paid sufficiently by the employers, and it was added to the cost of the meal, it would be much more satisfactory. However, I understand that many of these waiters receive little or nothing in return for their services, and have to depend largely upon the tips which they receive from their customers. In cases of that kind, they are entitled to something for their work. However, conditions vary in different places, and we have to take into consideration the local custom, and also one's own personal convictions. I am sure that if you use your own judgment in the matter, that this will please the Lord. Try to imagine you were the waitress, instead of the customer. Have you ever done that? It might help to answer your question.

128. What stand should Christian parents take concerning television in the home?

The problem of the Christian home and television is one of the most difficult to solve in our modern society. There is no question that the evils of television outweigh by many times what little good it may do educationally, religiously, or for innocent entertainment. Personally, I wish television had never been invented, and feel that it is a far greater instrument for evil than good. But television is here to stay, and we must face the problem.

If we cannot keep it out of our homes, then we must make the best of it. It is then up to Christian parents to so control it that the children will not be allowed to see things which would harm them. This is not easy, but it must be done. It is a matter which is squarely up to the parents to use sanctified discernment. The use or abuse of television will depend upon the spirituality of the individual, and "every man must be persuaded in his own mind." We cannot decide or judge another. Let each one be sure that he can submit his decision to the scrutiny of God.

129. My boy friend and I are both fourteen years old. Is it a sin for us to kiss?

I would say that you are still quite young to indulge in these intimacies with your fourteen-year-old friend. You are not yet old enough to recognize the seriousness of married life; and until you are absolutely sure that you have met the man with whom you expect to live, I believe that it is better to refrain from intimate relationships such as petting and kissing. While you may have only the purest motives, you still must be careful not to encourage temptations which may lead to major circumstances.

130. **My wife and I believe in eating only vegetable food, and we have been criticized by friends and people in our church. We have been offended by their setting meat before us when we have visited in their homes and no longer fellowship with them.**

There are honest differences of opinion among people, and we ought to respect one another's convictions in these matters. However, it is well to remember that we are always to be very charitable, and not try to force our convictions upon others who may not see things in the same way that we do. After all, the Lord Jesus Christ was not a strict vegetarian, but we read in Luke 24:42, 43 that He ate a piece of broiled fish, which of course, is not a vegetable. The Apostle Paul also does not condemn those who see no harm in eating meat, even meat which had been offered and sacrificed to idols. I suggest that you read very carefully the 8th chapter of I Corinthians. I would also call your attention to I Corinthians 10:25 where Paul tells us that:

> Whatsoever is sold in the shambles [butcher shop], that eat, asking no question for conscience sake (I Cor. 10:25).

In verse 27 he says if you are invited to a feast, you should eat "whatsoever is set before you, . . . asking no question for conscience sake." From these passages it is very evident that it is a matter of personal conviction, and we cannot force our own views upon others. In Romans 14 Paul says:

> For one believeth that he may eat all things: another, who is weak, eateth herbs.
> Let not him that eateth despise him that eateth not; and

let not him which eateth not judge him that eateth: for God hath received him (Rom. 14:2, 3).

If anyone feels that it is wrong to eat meat, he ought not to eat it, and he is none the worse for it. However, we must be careful that we do not judge others who do not feel the same way that we do. The wrong is not in holding our convictions, but the wrong is in becoming fanatical in these things, and trying to force our own personal beliefs on everybody else, and in that way we exclude ourselves from fellowship. I believe that we ought to have convictions, but they should never be made the occasion for the disruption of fellowship or for controversy about things which do not involve our salvation.

131. Is it right for a Christian to consider being cremated?

I have always felt that it was wrong for people to allow their bodies to be cremated. I do not know of any particular passage in Scripture which positively forbids it, but there is also nothing in the Bible which in any way would sanction it. The committal which God Himself gave was "dust thou art, and unto dust shalt thou return" (Gen. 3:19). He does not say that they shall return unto ashes, but unto dust. It has been the custom throughout the ages to bury the bodies of the deceased, and the practice of cremation is the result of infidelity and unbelief on the part of some. They suppose that in this way they could prevent the resurrection.

However, we do believe that God who made the world out of nothing and man out of the dust of the earth would have no more difficulty in reconstituting the body from ashes than He would from the other elements. Personally, I would not censure anyone if this were done in ignorance; however, I do not believe that instructed, Bible-loving Christians should follow these pagan customs, but rather practice that which was followed throughout the entire record of Scriptures.

132. Should the tithe be figured on the gross or the net income?

The question of tithing on net or gross income should be no problem. We can accept the definition which the government itself gives. The government taxes us on our net income; that is, we are taxed on the total of our real earnings. This is called the net income, and on that you pay your taxes to the government. I therefore believe that the net income on which the Lord expects the tithe plus the offering is our total receipts after business expenses, but before the income tax has been deducted. It certainly does not seem right that we should pay Uncle Sam first, and then figure the Lord's portion on what is left.

CHAPTER IX

DOCTRINAL QUESTIONS

133. What part does faith have in the matter of salvation?

Faith is essential in salvation. There is no salvation
without it. We must remember that while the new birth
is the work of God by His grace in our hearts, faith is the
hand with which we accept this gift of God. We cannot
separate believing and being born again, since they both
have to do with the same operation—God's part and our
part.

**134. Is it necessary to PRAY THROUGH for salvation?
I have heard others talk about this, but do not understand what they mean.**

There is nothing in the Bible which tells us that we
must "pray through" in order to be saved. This is a
human invention, and is designed to play upon the
emotions of people, and get them to break down until
they mistake emotional experience for a spiritual experience. It has nothing to do with salvation, since in
order to be saved we must "believe on the Lord Jesus
Christ," and accept Him as our personal Saviour. I know
that in certain groups great stress is laid upon emotions,
and while emotions are involved, it is faith which saves.

135. Please explain "sanctification" to me.

The word "sanctification" occurs in three senses in the Scriptures. First of all, *things* are said to be sanctified, such as altars, the Tabernacle, and days, which only means that they have been SET ASIDE for a specific purpose to the Lord.

Then too, there is a positional sanctification of every believer. The moment we trust the Lord Jesus Christ, we are not only justified, but also sanctified and "set apart" for Him in salvation.

Then there is a third aspect of sanctification in which we grow in grace and in the knowledge of the Lord Jesus Christ, attaining unto practical holiness as we go along. This is a progressive thing, which will not be completed until we reach the end of life. Complete, practical sanctification is accomplished at the end of our earthly journey.

If you will remember that the basic idea of sanctification (which comes from the same root word as "holiness") is a "setting apart for definite service," I think you will have the key to understanding the various ways in which the word is used in the Bible. Inanimate objects, and even buildings, are said to be sanctified when dedicated to the service of the Lord. Every believer is sanctified in Christ, and it is also true that these must be practically sanctified in their lives because of their relationship to the Saviour.

136. Is there a difference between "fornication" and "adultery," in the teaching of Matthew, chapters 5 and 19?

We cannot hang a doctrine or build a dogma on one or two isolated passages of Scripture, and so we have to take into consideration all of the teaching of the Word of God, and not only the 5th and 19th chapters of

Matthew to which you also refer. When we take all of the references to fornication and adultery in the Scriptures, we find that they all refer generally to the same sin of immorality and illicit cohabitation.

In general, the word "fornication" refers to the unmarried, while "adultery" has more of a definite reference to married people. But they both describe the same sin, and the Bible certainly does not make any difference between them.

137. Do you believe in a "universal" or a "limited" atonement? Please explain your reasoning.

This is one of the most misunderstood questions. In a certain sense both are true. I personally believe that Christ died on the Cross to atone for the sins of all men, but only those who receive His finished work are saved. In other words, we believe in a universal atonement, but that it avails only for those who avail themselves of its benefits by faith.

When Moses smote the rock in the wilderness, there was enough water for all the people, but it availed only for those who were willing to stoop down and drink. It is impossible to go into a detailed discussion of this in correspondence. However, I do believe that Christ died for all men, but each one must individually accept the work that He has accomplished.

138. I am a church member and thought that I was saved, but now I am concerned about my soul and don't know if I ever really was born again. Please help me.

You have undoubtedly been looking at yourself more than you have at the Saviour. Being a church member, of course, doesn't mean anything unless you are really trusting in the finished work of the Lord Jesus Christ.

In order to make this thing absolutely sure, so that there will be no doubts in your mind, why don't you right now get upon your knees and ask the Lord definitely to save you.

Then take your Bible and turn to Romans 10:13, and read very carefully the following promise of God: "Whosoever shall call upon the name of the Lord SHALL be saved." That is a definite statement in the Word of God, which you must believe. Since you have called upon Him, and asked Him to save you, you must now believe —believe that He also keeps His Word, and therefore you are saved, not because you feel it, or think so, but because the Word of God says so.

Then too, there is another Scripture in I John 5:1 which says, "Whosoever believeth that Jesus is the Christ is born of God." Now if you believe that Jesus is the Christ, then He says that you have been born of God. You must accept that, not because you can feel it, not because your reason tells you so, but because the Word of God is definite in this matter.

139. I am so troubled about my spiritual condition. I once thought I was saved and knew the joy of salvation, but sin has come into my life, and I am afraid that I have committed the unpardonable sin. Is there any hope for me?

> If we confess our sins, He is faithful and just to forgive us our sins, and to cleanse us from all unrighteousness (I John 1:9).

This is the unchangeable Word and promise of the living God. There is no mention made here of any sin which is not to be forgiven if we are willing to confess it. We must believe the Word of God, and believe that what He says is the truth, rather than listen to what man may say.

After all, the final thing on which we can base our eternal hope is the Word of the living God. After reading your letter, therefore, I thought I would remind you that you must put your hope and trust in this verse found in I John 1:9, and not in what you have heard people say, or even heard preachers preach. Remember that even preachers are not always infallible.

I realize that the Devil would like to rob you of the assurance of your salvation by putting all sorts of thoughts into your mind, but remember that you are saved by grace, not because of your own goodness, but in spite of your own unworthiness and sinfulness. If any of us, including myself, should stand on our own record, we would be forever lost. We must therefore cast ourselves entirely on the mercy and the grace of God, and then accept His promise of I John 1:9. If you have confessed your sin, then the Lord has forgiven you all your unrighteousness and iniquity.

Those who have committed the unpardonable sin are wholly unconscious of it. I do not believe that anybody who has really gone beyond the line even comes under conviction. The very fact that you are disturbed about it, shows that you have not committed any sin that the Lord will not forgive. Do not allow Satan to rob you of your assurance, but just keep quoting to him I John 1:9, and claim the promise, and you will find peace for your heart.

140. I am not so sure that I am prepared for eternity. How can I be sure?

After reading your letter I feel it is possible that you have the wrong idea about the matter of salvation. We are all by nature lost and under the condemnation of sin; but since we were totally helpless to lift even one single finger toward our own redemption, the Lord made provision in the person of the Lord Jesus Christ, whom He sent into the world to bear our human nature, to take upon Himself our sin, to carry it to the Cross, and to prove that redemption was completed by rising from the grave on the third day. Now salvation is simply the free gift of God, received by faith in the Lord Jesus Christ.

You are not to base your salvation upon your own judgment or reason, or your feelings or emotions, but entirely on the basis of faith in the Word of God. The Word of God cannot fail, and if we put our trust in the promises of God, we may rest assured that all is well with our soul. In Romans 10:13 we read:

> Whosoever shall call upon the name of the Lord shall be saved.

There are no "ifs" and "ands" about this verse, and since you have called upon the Lord for salvation, you may rest assured that He will keep His Word.

I do not know just what your difficulty is, whether you are looking for some kind of an emotion or feeling or other manifestation, but these things are not necessary. Salvation is a simple, childlike acceptance of the promises of God concerning the Lord Jesus Christ, and then trusting him implicitly in spite of everything else.

141. If the Spirit is withdrawn from the earth at the Rapture, how then will people be saved?

The Spirit will be withdrawn as the "indwelling Spirit" in the Body of Christ, but He will still be here as the omnipresent third person of the Trinity. After the Rapture, people will be saved just as they were in the Old Testament before Pentecost.

142. Who will be saved after the Rapture and during the Tribulation?

A multitude from every people, tribe, and nation will be saved during the Tribulation. Read Revelation 7:9,

> After this I beheld, and, lo, a great multitude, which no man could number, of all nations, and kindreds, and people, and tongues, stood before the throne, and before the Lamb, clothed with white robes, and palms in their hands (Rev. 7:9).

First God will save 144,000 of the twelve tribes of Israel (Rev. 7:4-8), and then the multitude of Gentiles (from all nations, kindreds, people, and tongues). These will be from among those who never heard the Gospel and had not deliberately rejected it. Those who had heard the Gospel message and willfully turned it down will not have another chance (II Thess. 2:10-12).

143. How could Jesus be sinless if he was born of a sinful woman?

The virgin birth is the answer. Sin is reckoned through the FATHER, not the mother. It was not Eve's sin which makes us "sinners by birth," but the sin of Adam. The sin of Adam as the federal head of the race is transmitted to us. It is passed down through the man, not the woman. Study carefully Romans 5:12, 17, 19.

> Wherefore, as by one man sin entered into the world, and death by sin; and so death passed upon all men, for that all have sinned:
> For as by one man's offence death reigned by one; much more they which receive abundance of grace and of the gift of righteousness shall reign in life by one, Jesus Christ.
> For as by one man's disobedience many were made sinners, so by the obedience of one shall many be made righteous (Rom. 5:12, 17, 19).

144. Are we by grace born again unto believing unto eternal life, or do we by grace believe unto re-birth unto eternal life?

This question is an old theological battleground. From the standpoint of God, a sinner cannot believe until after he is born again. According to the Word of God the sinner is "dead in trespasses and in sins" and therefore is unable to do anything until he has been given life. Therefore, the work of God in new birth is the first act, and then as a result of that, he believes on the Lord Jesus Christ. This is the Calvinistic approach to the matter of the new birth.

On the other hand, there are those who teach that when we believe we are then through that act born again, and therefore faith is the cause of the new birth rather than the result of the new birth.

There are godly and sincere men on both sides of the argument. Personally, I believe that salvation is of the Lord, and that the work of regeneration is entirely a divine operation, and therefore our faith is the evidence that we have already been chosen of God. Some of these things may not seem clear to us here, but we shall understand some day.

145. How can I know that I have the witness of the Spirit?

The Bible itself is the real witness of the Holy Spirit within our lives. We have no right to expect that we are going to hear any voices or see any strange sights to assure us that we belong to Him, but we are to believe God's Word, and in that way receive the witness of the Spirit. In I John 5, verse 9 we read:

> If we receive the witness of men, the witness of God is greater: for this is the witness of God which he hath testified of his Son.

> He that believeth on the son of God hath the witness in himself (I John 5:9, 10).

I would like to have you stop right here, and read that very carefully—"He that believeth on the Son of God hath the witness in himself." In other words, the requisite for the witness of the Spirit is to believe on the Son of God. And then the verse continues:

> . . . he that believeth not God hath made him a liar; because he believeth not the record that God gave of His Son.
>
> And this is the record, that God hath given to us eternal life, and this life is in His Son (I John 5:10, 11).

Will you notice carefully that the sin of rejecting Christ is unbelief concerning the RECORD that God gave of His Son. This record is found in the Bible, and we receive the witness of the Spirit when we believe what God has to say in the Word concerning His Son. Then we can put our finger on that promise and say, "God says it, and therefore it must be so." And then the Spirit witnesses through the Word that you are a child of God.

Take, for instance, Romans 10:13—"Whosoever shall call upon the name of the Lord shall be saved." If we take this verse and call upon the name of the Lord in sincerity and truth, then we have a right to claim that God promises us eternal life because we have called upon His name. You must realize that there is no witness of the Spirit apart from the Word of God, because the Word is the witness of the Spirit, and when we believe the Word and trust it, then the Spirit witnesses with our spirit through the Bible.

Maybe you have confused the witness of the Spirit with some kind of a feeling or sensation or emotion. We must believe God's Word, whether we feel it or not, and then the Spirit will witness with our spirit.

146. What is the unpardonable sin?

The Bible does not use the term, "unpardonable sin." It is usually confused with "blasphemy against the Holy Ghost" (Matthew 12:31):

> . . . All manner of sin and blasphemy shall be forgiven unto men: but the blasphemy against the Holy Ghost shall not be forgiven unto men.
>
> And whosoever speaketh a word against the Son of man, it shall be forgiven him: but whosoever speaketh against the Holy Ghost, it shall not be forgiven him, neither in this world, neither in the world to come (Matt. 12:31, 32).

This was a sin the Nation of Israel committed, and does not apply to this dispensation of grace. There is also a "sin unto death" which only believers can commit:

> If any man see his brother sin a sin which is not unto death, he shall ask, and he shall give him life for them that sin not unto death. There is a sin unto death: I do not say that he shall pray for it (I John 5:16).

It does not involve the question of salvation, but chastening of the Lord (I Cor. 11:32). There is only one sin which cannot be forgiven, and that is continued rejection of Jesus UNTIL IT IS TOO LATE. Anyone who receives Christ will be saved.

147. How can we be members of the "Body of Christ" and yet still be the "Bride of Christ"?

The Body of Christ consists of all members of the true Church since Pentecost. They are *positionally* joined to their Head, and said to be IN CHRIST and Christ IN THEM. It is the closest possible union. IN HIM we are already "seated in the heavenlies" (Eph. 2:6). This Body, the Church, will become the BRIDE of Christ after the Rapture and the Judgment Seat of Christ, when the Wedding of the Lamb takes place (Rev. 19).

According to the Word of God, Israel is the "wife" of Jehovah, while the Church will be the Bride of the Lord Jesus Christ. I believe that this is made perfectly clear in Ephesians, chapter 5, where the Church is not only compared to the members of the Body, but also as a Bride. The 32nd verse is all-conclusive, where it says,

> This is a great mystery: but I speak concerning Christ and the church (Eph. 5:32).

This refers back to Paul's revelation concerning the Church as the Body of Christ, as well as the Bride of Christ. In II Corinthians 11:2 Paul says concerning the Church,

> . . . I have espoused you to one husband . . . (II Cor. 11:2).

This, it seems to me, ought to settle the matter entirely. When the Lord created Eve He brought her to Adam, and Adam said, "this is bone of my bone, and flesh of my flesh" signifying that she was part of his body, and his bride as well. The statement, "they shall be one flesh," is spoken, of course, of the husband and the bride.

148. I am saved, but when do I lose the guilty conscience? Or is that the penalty? I am still afraid of the Lord's return, and cannot sleep because there seems no relief. How can I tell others of the joy that Christ brings when I have not experienced it?

To lose a guilty conscience over the past, you must exercise your faith in the promise of forgiveness as contained in the Word of God.

> If we confess our sins, he is faithful and just to forgive us our sins, and to cleanse us from all unrighteousness (I John 1:9).

We must accept this as a fact, and believe that God

has cleansed us, and be willing to pay whatever penalty is attached to the mistakes of the past.

I do not, however, believe that this should result in a guilty conscience, but rather in a submission to His will. If because of some things that have transpired in the past, we have to carry the scars for awhile down here, we should take it graciously, but accept His forgiveness in all sincerity. After all, if the Lord says that He has forgiven and cleansed you from all unrighteousness, you should in faith accept it, and not allow yourself to be troubled by a sense of guilt which the Lord has completely taken away upon confession of your sin.

Chapter X

MARRIAGE, DIVORCE, AND RE-MARRIAGE

149. Does the Bible permit the re-marriage of a divorced person after the other party has died?

There is nothing in the Bible which prohibits the re-marriage of a person after their first mate has been taken away by death. I believe that the 7th chapter of Romans, verses 2 and 3, make this quite clear:

> For the woman which hath an husband is bound by the law to her husband so long as he liveth; but if the husband be dead, she is loosed from the law of her husband.
>
> So then if, while her husband liveth, she be married to another man, she shall be called an adulteress: but if her husband be dead, she is free from the law; so that she is no adulteress, though she be married to another man (Rom. 7:2, 3).

If you ask, "Does the death of this one now justify the sins of the past?" the answer is, "Of course not!" But as far as Scripture goes, death dissolves the relationship, and I see nothing which would prevent the remaining party from being re-married. Of course, the sins of the past would have to be confessed, and if possible rectified; but beyond this, nothing can be done.

150. What should be the position of a divorced person in the church fellowship, and what stand should the church take concerning their place in the work?

There are many different aspects and complications in this divorce problem, and so many circumstances have to be dealt with individually, that we, therefore, cannot give a blanket ruling as to what the conduct of a church should be in regard to the matter of the service of divorced people. Every case has to be decided on its own merit, and of course that is up to the board of the church to do.

However, I can give you my personal opinion. If people have made the mistake of being divorced and re-married, which is contrary to Scripture, and then see their error and are truly repentant and sorry, I believe that we ought to forgive them, for I believe that the Lord Himself would do the same thing. We therefore should not exclude them from our fellowship, but seek to help and encourage them in every possible way.

However, this is as far as I believe it ought to go, not because we do not fully forgive them, but because of the testimony before the world. I do not feel that people who have this stigma upon their past ought to be allowed to hold any prominent position in the church, but should take a subordinate place, and carry on their testimony without any more display than necessary. This is not because we do not forgive them, and do not love them, but because the world does not forgive and forget, and they might take offense at this. I believe that when people are truly repentant, and sorry for their sin, that they will be willing to pay the price, and for the sake of the testimony before the world, take a subordinate position in order that no one may be able to point a finger at the church, either rightly or wrongly. We ought to guard ourselves from every appearance of evil.

This is a very complex thing, and we ought to be very,

very careful not to become a reproach before the world, and I am sure that those who seek to serve the Lord should be willing to give up their own liberties and rights, if need be, for the good of the testimony of the Gospel of Christ.

151. Does the Bible give us the details of the ceremony which must be used at a wedding?

There is no verse in the Bible of any kind that deals with this matter. In olden times, when a man and a woman promised their devotion to each other, they were considered to be married, and their engagement could not be broken. The ceremony part has only come in as a legal aspect to prevent the abuse, because of man's sinfulness.

152. Should people divorced and then re-married be allowed to take of the Lord's Supper?

Concerning the privilege of people who have been divorced and re-married to sit at the Lord's Table, this depends entirely on whether the sin has been confessed and forsaken, or whether they continue in unrepentant sin. Of course, if a person has been divorced on Scriptural grounds, there is nothing to prevent them from partaking of the Lord's Table, since the Lord in His teaching definitely tells us that divorce is permitted on grounds of fornication and adultery. However, we cannot refuse people to come to the Lord's Table, because it is a matter between themselves and the Lord. I think that I Corinthians 11:28 will answer your question:

> Let a man examine HIMSELF: so let him eat of that bread and drink of that cup (I Cor. 11:28).

This is a matter between the individual and the Lord.

153. Our church has called a pastor who was divorced on unscriptural grounds, and has been re-married. We are not in accord with calling him, and would like your opinion in this matter.

Personally, I think that such a pastor is not in a position to preach the whole counsel of God, for he certainly would not have liberty to preach on subjects such as marriage and divorce and re-marriage and home relationships, since immediately folk will begin pointing their finger at him.

In the service of the Temple and the Tabernacle, according to Leviticus, chapter 21, verses 16 to 24, the priest was to be without blemish. If he had any serious blemish, he was considered to be a crippled priest, and therefore was not allowed to serve in the highest office of the priesthood. I believe that there are many "crippled priests" among us today, and while I do not know all the circumstances in your case, I do feel that it would hinder a man's ministry greatly if he had a record of an unscriptural divorce and re-marriage. However, if the church feels that they did right in calling him, I do not see that there is anything that you personally can do about it. What course to follow under these conditions will have to be decided between you and the Lord. May He grant you wisdom in these difficult decisions.

154. I am divorced from my husband who is not a Christian. Since my divorce, I have been saved. He never re-married, and now wants to marry me again. Does the Bible give any light as to what action I should take concerning this?

Concerning taking back your husband after all you have gone through, this is a matter entirely between

yourself and the Lord. Of course, if you have Scriptural
grounds for divorce, there is nothing we can say, and
you need not take him back while still unsaved; but if you
have enough love and grace in your heart, so that you
can overlook the past, and put up with him in the hope
and the prayer that God will eventually save him, so
much to your credit, and I believe that it would be honoring to the Lord.

I am not telling you to do this, because it is not my
business to decide, but only tell you what I believe the
will of the Lord is. I repeat, if you have enough grace
and patience to take him back, I am sure that the Lord
would honor that faith, and eventually save your husband. If you feel that for the sake of the family and himself you can give him another try, I am sure that no one
could object.

155. **I have been divorced and my wife is still living. I have
met a Christian girl whom I would like to marry.
Someone told me that you would not perform the
ceremony under these circumstances, and so I would
like to know if you would, and if not, why?**

In all such cases we must abide by the clear teaching of
the Word. We must remember that we cannot be moti-
vated by our sentiments, or our feelings, or what we would
like to see or do. As such I do not believe that there is
anything in the Word of God whatsoever to suggest that
a person who has been divorced is permitted to re-marry
while both parties to the contract are still alive. If we
would open the door ever so little, it would result in
everybody finding some excuse for re-marriage, because
everyone has some method of justifying his own position.

In regard to your direct question, whether I would

marry you to a real Christian girl, while your first wife is still alive, my answer is an absolute, positive NO! I realize that this would not prevent you from getting married, if you so desired, because there are many others who would be happy to do so; but I cannot conscientiously do it, because I believe that I would be violating the clear teaching of the Word of God. Some day I shall have to stand before the Judgment Seat of Christ and give an account of what I do, and I do not want any of these things on my hands.

156. I have heard that the innocent party to a divorce may re-marry.

The mistake that you, and so many others make is that you would base your conclusion on one or two isolated passages in Scripture, while I believe that all the Scriptures are to be taken together, and then the general sense of all of them has to be taken as the conclusion. I am sure that if we leave the door open only a quarter of an inch for divorced people to crawl through, and become re-married on the condition that they are the innocent party, we might just as well open all the flood gates, for everyone then would be able to justify themselves and argue that they were the innocent party. In fact, I have met very, very few people in my long ministerial career who ever admitted that they were guilty. I therefore am going to stick to the conservative side, and keep the door closed, because I believe that this is much safer than leaving it open even a fraction of an inch. God alone knows who the innocent party is.

157. Should Negroes and Whites inter-marry?

In regard to your question concerning the Negro race, we must realize that the inadvisability of inter-marriage

between Negroes and Whites is not because of any difference in their origin or color, but only because the
Negro has not had the opportunity the white man has
had over many centuries to attain the social level which
we feel is necessary for a happy marriage. I do not believe that there should be inter-marriage among these
widely different groups any more than there should be
inter-marriage among people who differ widely in their
religious beliefs, such as Catholics and Protestants, and
other ones. This is the only reason I know for not endorsing it.

There is such a wide gulf between Negroes and Whites
in the matter of emotions, behaviorism, sentiments, as
well as habits and appetites, that inter-marriage con-
stitutes an "unequal yoke."

**158. I was divorced and have been re-married. The Lord
has now convicted me of this sin, and I wonder what
I am to do about it.**

You have a real problem, and I do not know what to
say, since this is a matter that you must settle between
yourself and the Lord. While the Lord forgives, we
must also remember that we reap what we sow, and we
oftentimes have to pay the penalty for it. I realize that
some of these questions simply cannot be answered, because after the evil has been done, it is hard to undo it
again. I am sure that if you wait on the Lord, He will
direct you, and tell you what to do.

**159. If a person marries and divorces on grounds of adultery
while unsaved, and then later re-marries and accepts
Christ, and feels the call to the ministry, is he eligible
for ordination?**

In regard to a divorced person serving in the ministry,

it is impossible for us to lay down any hard and fast rules, since the Bible does not clearly give its answer on these things. Since this man was divorced before he was saved and knew the truth, I do believe that the Lord forgives and forgets. However, people do not always forget, and he is likely to find his ministry sharply limited because of this past history. People are not always as eager to forget as the Lord is. However, I believe that this is a matter that should be taken care of by the local church, and we cannot generalize on this particular situation. I think it would be up to the individual group and ordination council to decide whether an ordination should be performed. I believe that all these matters have to be considered individually.

If a man is saved after making the mistake, and sees and confesses his fault, I would be the last one to put up a hindrance to his ministry.

160. In the Old Testament we read many instances of polygamy. Was this permissible under the Old Testament law?

Concerning polygamy in the Old Testament, you must remember that God PERMITTED the Old Testament saints to have more than one wife, but He NEVER SANCTIONED it, and in every case it was followed by disaster and tragedy.

161. Here is my problem: A friend of mine a few years ago was dating a girl in whom he had no special interest. One thing led to another, and she became pregnant. He married her to give the child a name. They were divorced immediately. It is my understanding that they never lived as man and wife. What saith the

Scriptures? He found Christ about a year after this episode.

This is indeed a tragic situation, and presents a great many problems, but as I see the Word of God, there was absolutely no excuse for this friend of yours who married the mother of his child, to then abandon both his wife and child. I certainly feel that he cannot be justified on the excuse that he claims that they never lived as man and wife. Certainly they must have lived as man and wife if she became pregnant by him (even though prior to the legal marriage), and I feel it is his duty to take care of her as well as the child. I believe that since he found the Lord Jesus Christ as his Saviour, he ought to make every effort to make restitution as far as is possible. The fact that he did it before he was saved, of course, is put under the blood, but it does not relieve him of the responsibility.

Chapter XI

MEDICAL PROBLEMS

162. I am studying for the ministry, am married and have two children. A larger family would work a considerable hardship on us financially, and I would like your opinion on the matter of a vasectomy for myself.

You would be committing a great sin by being sterilized. I do not feel that the reason you give for not wanting a larger family is one which is valid, and one which you can conscientiously give to the Lord. You state that you feel that any more children "would work a considerable hardship on us financially." Certainly if the Lord wants you to have more children, He will also make it possible for you to care for them in the proper way. I therefore feel that you are not in the will of the Lord in your position, and to have an artificial sterilization performed would be definitely contrary to the will of the Lord, and could result in nothing else but displeasure and the judgment of the Lord, since there is absolutely no basis for any such act in the Scriptures. I hope that the Lord will show you that this would be an improper act, and that He will give you grace to believe that whatever is His will for you in the matter of a family, He also will provide.

163. I have read several articles in magazines concerning artificial insemination for childless couples. Do you think we would be going contrary to the Lord's will in submitting to this?

Becoming the mother of another man's child, instead of your own husband's, certainly cannot be defended. I personally cannot see that this is ever to be practiced among believers. Even though the husband agreed, it could never be the same between him and his wife, and I am afraid that it would leave a very bad impression, and might have serious consequences. I fear that the consciousness of the fact that this was not your husband's own child could have some very bad effect later on. As far as I can see from the Word of God, we ought to continue to seek the will of the Lord in the natural course of events, and not in this artificial method whatsoever. I would suggest that you try and adopt a child into your home, which would be a far better solution than the one which you suggest.

164. I do not see how following the pattern set forth in the 15th Chapter of Leviticus results in birth control. I would like to have a better explanation of this.

Concerning birth control, you must remember that the only Scriptural birth control revealed in the Word of God is self-control. This is the only way the Lord has given of controlling the number of children, and there is no authority in the Bible at all for the use of artificial or mechanical means and contraceptives. In the 15th chapter of Leviticus we have, of course, the rule of abstinence during certain periods of the cycle which, if followed carefully, will not result in NO children, but will result in the spacing of the children according to the will of God. So many people have the mistaken idea that the Bible teaches in this chapter the PREVEN-TION of conception, but it does nothing of the kind. It is rather birth CONTROL, but NOT birth PRE-VENTION. I believe that if Christians, who want to do the will of the Lord in obedience to Him and raise a family according to His own command, will follow these injunctions, that then the Lord Himself will undertake not only to space the children and regulate the number, but give the grace and the means to take care of those He sends to them. The trouble today is that Christians dare not trust the Lord, but take it into their own hands and means, and the result is this tragic condition of our youth because our families are planned by man instead of by God.

The sad part is that many of our good physicians in the country today do not look at this matter at all from a Scriptural standpoint, and therefore their advice is often-times only from the material standpoint and does not take into consideration the fact that God honors those that dare to trust Him and honor Him.

I believe that born-again Christians, if they are well and healthy, ought to look to the Lord only for the solution of this problem, and I know they will not be disappointed. We must remember that according to Scripture, children are a blessing of the Lord, and the greater the number, the greater the blessing.

165. I have read in the Book of Leviticus concerning puri-fication after childbirth, and wonder if this is Old Testament law or applies as well today.

Concerning the laws of purification after childbirth as given in the Book of Leviticus, I believe that for sanitary reasons they still hold for us today, and that the Lord expects that we shall observe these days of abstinence and purification after a child has been born. This is not only for sanitary reasons, but also for reasons of health. The principle still holds, even though offerings and sacrifices and other legal restrictions given in the Bible do not apply today. However, I do believe that we ought to observe the general principle of these things, and the Lord Himself will bless us.

166. Is nervousness the work of Satan? My pastor said if a person had Christ they would have no trouble with their nerves. I know that I belong to the Lord, and yet sometimes I am very nervous.

Don't believe everything your pastor says, especially on matters he knows little about. I am so sorry that someone has completely misinformed you as to the source of nerves. It is absolutely not true at all that nervousness is the work of Satan. Nervousness is only another form of disease affecting the nerves instead of other organs; and while it is very distressing, we believe that the Lord understands this as well as all other sicknesses. I hope that you will not allow yourself to be disturbed by those who do not understand these things and say things which only add to your grief instead of helping you.

167. Is giving one's body for medical experiment in the interest of science contrary to the teaching of God's Word?

I take it that you are referring to making your corpse available after your death for scientific research. "Willing" your body for laboratory experiments in the interest of science is a personal matter which has to be decided by the individual, and we cannot legislate in this matter for someone else. Personally, I believe that the Scriptural method of disposition of the body is by burial, and there is no evidence in the Bible that cremation or other methods are tolerated.

However, I think that we must make a distinction. If cremation is practiced with the idea of preventing a resurrection, of course, this is an evidence of unbelief, and is dishonoring to the Lord. In the case of giving your body for the progress of science, I think it is quite different. You will have to settle that with the Lord; but I do not believe that it is necessary in your case, unless there is something of a special interest which might help science in finding out things which could not be found out in other cases. There are many, many bodies of unidentified people, which can be worked upon, and unless it is of a special significance, I do not believe that your body would be of any particular help. I certainly do not see any sense in routine autopsies, but in the case of a rare or unusual disease, a post mortem might help some other sufferer.

168. Is cancer a disease the Lord puts upon one who lives in unconfessed sin?

It COULD be the judgment of God upon unconfessed sin, but not necessarily so. We believe that the statement in I Corinthians 11 concerning sickness and weakness does not refer to any one particular disease, but refers to sickness in general. Therefore, when the Lord visits His people in chastening, it is not necessarily any one particular kind of illness, but may be almost anything. There is no reason to suppose that cancer is an exception, nor to say that cancer is the result of unconfessed sin.

Of course, we know that the Lord is able to heal, but we must pray always in the will of the Lord. Even our Lord Jesus Christ when He faced the Cross, prayed "not My will, but Thy will be done." And so whenever we ask the Lord to do anything for us, we must be sure that we meet two conditions: it must be Scriptural, and it must be His will.

169. Would a Christian woman be going ahead of the Lord by taking shots to make her stronger, in order to become pregnant?

First of all, you must pray about it, and then I do not see any reason in the world why you should not use all the available means which medical science has of relieving your sterility. Where there is some physical reason why you do not become pregnant, and it can be relieved, I believe that it is the will of the Lord that you should do so. Sometimes this can be relieved by a simple operation and sometimes by giving certain medicines, either by mouth or hypodermically or intramuscularly. Whichever method is used makes no difference, but if the doctors do have a remedy for your condition which would not in any way endanger your health, I am sure that there could be no objection whatsoever. I do not know of anything in the Bible which would prevent you from doing so. But before you consult the doctor, read Genesis 25:21,

> And Isaac intreated the LORD for his wife, because she was barren: and the LORD was intreated of him, and Rebekah his wife conceived (Gen. 25:21).

I can easily understand your desire to have a family, especially as the years slip by, and so my advice would be that you follow the advice of your doctor, and then leave the thing entirely with the Lord, believing that whatever He may be pleased to do will be best for you.

170. I heard someone make the statement that disease was a work of the Devil and the result of demon possession. I would like your opinion of this.

Disease is the result of sin, but to say that all sickness is the work of the Devil is a false and dangerous statement. This claim is made by a great many ignorant people who do not know the Word of the Lord, and by professional racketeering "healers" who are trying to promote some racket of their own. If I were you, I would pay absolutely no attention to them whatsoever. There is nothing in the Bible to indicate that the Devil is the cause of any particular disease, although the Lord may permit Satan to chasten God's people for some unconfessed sin.

When Lazarus died, in the 11th chapter of John, the Lord Jesus Christ said:

> . . . This sickness is not unto death, but for the glory of God, that the Son of God might be glorified thereby (John 11:4).

We believe that sometimes the Lord permits us to be ill in order that He may bring out in us certain qualities which could not be developed in any other way. We know, for instance, that—

> . . . tribulation worketh patience;
> And patience, experience; and experience, hope:
> And hope maketh not ashamed; because the love of God
> is shed abroad in our hearts by the Holy Ghost which is
> given unto us (Rom. 5:3-5).

I would therefore pay absolutely no attention to the charge of those who would have you believe that this is the work of Satan or the result of demon possession.

It is utterly unscriptural, without any grounds, and is made by irresponsible persons who ought to know better.

171. I would like to know since you are an M. D., what you think of these highly advertised healing campaigns which are being carried on. Someone told me to stay away because it was of the Devil.

I think that most of these highly advertized healing programs are a fake from start to finish, and there is absolutely nothing of the Spirit of God in it at all. I do not know how much the Devil has to do with it, but I am sure that it is a thing of the flesh, and not of the Lord. If these people really could heal the way they claim they are healing, they certainly would not have to be begging for money all the time; and yet this is one of the disturbing characteristics of their program. Certainly if they had the power of healing as they constantly affirm, people in gratitude would be willing to pour their thousands and even millions into their coffers for the sake of being healed. This alone should put a question in our minds as to the legitimacy of their claims.

Personally, I believe that the special signs of healing were apostolic signs, and ceased with the age of the apostles. They will not re-appear as gifts to individuals until after the Church is gone, and God begins to deal again with Israel. The signs and miracles belong to the Nation of Israel and not to the Church. Paul tells us:

> For the Jews require a sign, and the Greeks seek after wisdom:
> But we preach Christ crucified (I Cor. 1:22, 23).

I believe it is our business to keep on preaching a crucified Christ, and forget about all these other things. However, I do not doubt for one moment that Satan has the power under certain limitations to perform miracles, and probably even to heal. Of course, this is only by permission of the Lord.

We should add only one note of explanation and that is that we know that the Lord is able to heal if it be His will. The Lord heals in answer to prayer, and I know of many instances even in my own family where the Lord has healed in answer to the prayer of faith; but what I have said applies only to these public, unscriptural meetings with all the ballyhoo and trappings of Hollywood and the world. The methods used certainly have no precedent whatsoever in the Scriptures.

172. How do you account for the birth of twins, triplets, and quadruplets, and their apparent increase in these days?

Concerning the birth of twins, triplets, and quadruplets, this is a genetic matter which science has tried to explain. It is quite an involved study, and there is a great deal of literature which has been written on it, but even science is not too sure just exactly what causes identical twins and triplets. It is quite a study, and a great deal of work is being done along that line. I must confess that I am not entirely clear on the matter myself. I certainly do not know how to account for the apparent increase in multiple births in these last days.

173. I do not agree with you concerning your stand on divine healing. I feel that it belongs to this dispensation just as it did during the apostolic days.

I believe that God can heal, but I do not believe that the gift of divine healing is committed to individuals as it was in the days of the apostles. These were apostolic gifts, and included not only healing of the bodies, but

walking on the water, raising the dead, cleansing the
lepers, and things of that kind. If some of these are for
us, then all of them must be there. The Lord performed
many, many miracles while He was here upon the
earth, and the apostles were also given this power, but
that was for that special time and for a special need.

Again let me tell you that I do believe that God
can and does heal, but I do not believe that it is the rule
today; and the many, many reports which are being
made by those who claim to have a special commission
cannot stand up in the light of Scripture. Let me remind
you of one thing: when Jesus was here upon the earth,
and the apostles, they healed ALL that came to them.
There were no failures among them, but every one of
them was successful. This certainly cannot be said for
modern-day healers. Then too, concerning the passage
in James 5:13-16:

> Is any among you afflicted? let him pray. Is any merry? let
> him sing psalms.
> Is any sick among you? let him call for the elders of the
> church; and let them pray over him, anointing him with
> oil in the name of the Lord:
> And the prayer of faith shall save the sick, and the Lord
> shall raise him up; and if he have committed sins, they shall
> be forgiven him.
> Confess your faults one to another, and pray for one an-
> other, that ye may be healed. The effectual fervent prayer
> of a righteous man availeth much (James 5:13-16).

Here he is speaking about a specific kind of sickness
which was the result of unconfessed sin, and therefore
he links up the healing with the forgiveness of sins, and
the confession of faults. Of course, this has nothing to
do with divine healing meetings, but in this case the
elders are to go to the individual and to anoint him with

oil. There is no resemblance between the healings in the Bible and the methods used today by many.

174. My aged father who loves the Lord is a victim of leukemia. I am keeping it from him. Would you say I'm doing the right thing? Matters like this puzzle me. I pray but still can't be sure if I am doing the will of the Lord.

Without knowing all the facts, it is difficult to know what to say. We can only advise you and tell you what we feel we would do under the circumstances. Since he is saved and knows the Lord, I do not see that there is any point in telling him about the seriousness of his condition, since I do not feel that it would serve any good purpose. I would therefore not let him know about the leukemia condition unless I felt very definitely led of the Lord for some good reason to do so. The question of whether to tell him or not would also depend on your father's emotional and temperamental makeup. The shock might do more harm than you suspect.

175. A friend of mine suffering from cancer is considering going to the Hoxey Clinic. I have heard reports concerning this treatment and am wondering if it is advisable.

I am not in a position to speak with authority, since I have not personally investigated its claims. There is a great deal of difference of opinion as to the value of the treatment. I realize that there are many who give testimony to the fact that they have been helped, but I also know of a great many who have gone there and have received no help whatsoever, and some cases where the delay had very serious after-effects. The fact that there are a great many testimonies of healing does not always mean anything. Christian Science also claims a great many miraculous healings, and of course we put no faith in them at all. There is not a nostrum, patent medicine, or healing racket which cannot produce testimonies of healing.

Government agencies who reportedly have made a thorough investigation, have found the Hoxey treatment to be of no specific value, and the medical profession has never endorsed it.

176. Can a baby be marked before it is born, due to the mother being frightened?

Concerning the possibility of a baby being marked before birth because of a fright suffered on the part of the mother while she is carrying the baby, there is no basis for any such occurrence. It is entirely a superstition, and has no scientific backing.

177. I read about an accident where a patient was undergoing surgery and while on the operating table the heart stopped for a few minutes and then started again. Where does the soul go for those few minutes?

When the heart stops temporarily, the soul does not leave the body. It is merely a cessation of the heart beat, but life does not actually cease. There are many people who have skipping of the heart, skipping two or three beats, and it is possible for the heart to stop beating for several minutes without life departing. These are matters that we will know better when we get to Glory.

178. I was saved when a young boy, but while in service I backslid. I caught a venereal disease but was cured immediately. I have asked the Lord to forgive me and know that His "blood cleanseth from all sin."

However, I have read that diseases of this type can cause children to be born crippled and blind. I should like to marry and have a family, but am afraid that my children might suffer for my sin. I am greatly troubled about this and would appreciate your help and advice.

I know that you understand that if you have confessed your sin to the Lord, He is faithful and just to forgive (I John 1:9). There is therefore nothing to worry about, but you ought to forget the past, and press on for the Lord and make up for the lost time.

In regard to your past infection with a venereal disease, you need not let this disturb you, since today medicine has a complete cure for this disease. I would suggest that you have a periodic examination by a good physician, and if nothing shows up, you need not hesitate for one moment to enter into the responsibilities of family life. If the disease has been thoroughly treated and cured, there is no possibility of it being transmitted to the children.

179. I have often wondered why you left the medical profession to go into the ministry.

The answer is very simple. When the Lord saved me as a successful practicing physician and surgeon, I immediately felt the call to the full-time ministry of the Word of God, and could not find rest or peace until I had made the complete surrender. I believe that this was in answer to the prayers of my godly mother who had dedicated me early in life to the ministry of the Gospel. Of course, my medical training and practice has stood me in good stead, and has been a great help to me in the ministry.

180. Should a Christian submit himself to medical or dental hypnosis, not as a performance for entertainment, but in place of an anesthetic? Is it wrong to submit to the hypnotic power of a dentist or doctor any more than to submit to the power of an anesthetic? Is hypnosis a demonic power?

Concerning hypnosis, I do not personally believe that it is anything supernatural or Satanic. I have never found any evidence that it was of a Satanic or Devilish nature.

However, hypnosis is still in the experimental stage, and it is not generally accepted as a substitute for anesthesia. For general medical and dental anesthesia, I believe that the old anesthetics are still much more reliable than hypnosis. It is not yet determined just exactly what effect hypnosis may have upon the mentality of those who are subjected to it. We will need to have some more information and more demonstrations of a scientific nature before it can be generally accepted. However, I do not believe that subjecting to hypnosis necessarily causes a Christian to give place to demon powers. If it is done by qualified and trained doctors, there should be no danger. Only when tried by persons with insufficient knowledge is it a dangerous procedure.

181. A young man in my Sunday School class has confided in me and needs help concerning a personal problem, and since you are a physician as well as a Bible teacher I wonder if you could give me some advice on the matter of masturbation.

There is a great deal of difference of opinion on this matter. The Bible does not state this in any definite terms or spell it out in detail. It is usually understood that it is a normal reaction, but for a Christian it is possible to have victory over these passions as well. I believe that you ought to advise this young man that it is more honoring for him to overcome this temptation and trust the Lord to give him the victory, so that in the event that he should ever get married, there would be no complex due to a memory of abuses.

182. Someone told me that the fluorine they put in water is poison, and if this is true, shouldn't something be done to prevent it?

Concerning the matter of adding fluorine to the water, I do not believe that it is a poison in the minute quantity required, and I am sure that those who are in a position of authority will be very careful and not allow anything harmful to take place. The Public Health Departments are doing quite a little experimentation along this line, and it does seem to help children as far as their tooth decay is concerned. I am sure that if there were any real danger, the government would not allow it to continue.

183. Does the Bible teach divine healing?

Most assuredly! God does heal in answer to prayer, IF IT IS ACCORDING TO HIS WILL. We believe in divine healing, but we DO NOT believe in so-called "divine healers." The gift of healing as a special gift is not for today, and anyone who claims this "apostolic" gift is either deceived or a deceiver. If you will compare the incidents of healing by Jesus and the apostles with the utterly unscriptural, high-powered, commercialized methods employed by modern-day healers, you will soon detect that they are "fakes" and false prophets. Just because they preach the Gospel does not make them disciples

of Christ. Read carefully the words of Jesus in Matthew
7:21-23,

> Not every one that saith unto me, Lord, Lord, shall enter
> into the kingdom of heaven; but he that doeth the will of
> my Father which is in heaven.
>
> Many will say to me in that day, Lord, Lord, have we not
> prophesied in thy name? and in thy name have cast out
> devils? and in thy name done many wonderful works?
>
> And then will I profess unto them, I never knew you: de-
> part from me, ye that work iniquity (Matt. 7:21-23).

CHAPTER XII

MISCELLANEOUS QUESTIONS

184. Should we confess our sins and ask forgiveness, or only confess, since God has already forgiven?

This is a matter of "splitting hairs." In I John 1:9 we are told, of course, that "if we confess our sins, he is faithful and just to forgive." Here it tells us that if we confess, the Lord forgives. However, I do not see where there is any harm in asking the Lord to forgive us our sins, which in itself is a confession that we have sinned.

185. Does God always answer our prayers?

Yes, the Lord ALWAYS answers believing prayer. He never fails when we come to Him in faith. But the Lord does not always answer our prayers in the same way or at the time that we desire. God is infinitely wise and sometimes finds it necessary to answer our petitions in the negative, and say to us, "No, my child, what you ask for is not good for you, and I will have to refuse your request, but by-and-by you will understand the reason for it all."

186. What is the difference between the Temple and the Synagogue?

The Temple was the one and only place in Israel where sacrifices were permitted to be offered, and where the priests ministered. The synagogues were meeting places for the gathering of the people for worship, prayer, and the studying of the Scriptures. The synagogues came into use during the period between the Book of Malachi in the Old Testament and Matthew of the New Testament.

187. What is the difference between a Nazarite and a Nazarene?

A "Nazarite" was a person (either man or woman) who was wholly dedicated to the exclusive service of God. The word itself means "separated." A Nazarite was to touch no wine, never cut or shave the hair or beard, and never touch a dead body. For the law of the Nazarite read Numbers, chapter 6.

A Nazarene was a person who lived in Nazareth. He was called a Nazarene, just as we speak of a New Yorker or a Bostonian or a Londoner. Jesus was a Nazarene because He lived in Nazareth (Matt. 2:23).

188. Where in the Bible can I find the record of the three kings who followed the star to the stable in Bethlehem?

You will not be able to find this information anywhere in the Bible. It is a mere tradition. The Bible tells us of wise men who were led by a star to a HOUSE in Bethlehem (Matthew 2). Nowhere is it stated in the Bible that they were "kings" but wise men. Neither is the number given. It may have been two or three or four or more, and they did not find Jesus in a stable, but in a house:

> And when they were come into the HOUSE, they saw the young child with Mary his mother, and fell down, and worshipped him: and when they had opened their treasures,

they presented unto him gifts; gold, and frankincense, and myrrh (Matt. 2:11).

189. I heard a preacher say that Abraham was not a Jew. I had always believed he was the first Jew, and all Jews were descendants of Abraham.

All Jews are descendants of Abraham but Abraham himself was not a Jew. When God called him he was an Assyrian, and became a Hebrew, after he had "crossed over" from Ur of the Chaldees to Canaan. The word "Hebrew" simply means "one who crossed over." Hence all of Abraham's descendants are Hebrews. Jacob was the first Israelite. His name was changed from Jacob to Israel in Genesis 32:28. Hence all of Jacob's descendants are both Hebrews and Israelites. The name "Jew" was later applied particularly to the remnant who returned from the Babylonian captivity because they were mostly members of the southern kingdom of Judah. The word "Jew" means a "Juda-ite." All Jews are therefore Hebrews and Israelites as well.

190. If the law was given to the Jews, how could the Gentiles be saved in the Old Testament?

It is true that God has only one way of salvation, and while Israel was under the law, people were still saved by faith. Abraham was saved by faith, although he lived four hundred years before the law came. In Hebrews 11 we have the record of Abel, Enoch, Noah, and all the other saints of God who were saved just as we are; they, by looking forward to the time when the Lord Jesus Christ would come in fulfillment of all the prophecies, while we look BACK to that event.

Gentiles, of course, could be saved, but they had to come by way of the true God, Jehovah of Israel. Therefore, a Gentile who was taken into the company of the Nation of Israel became a proselyte. He had to be circumcised and had to submit himself to all the religious ritual of that day. That was God's own way of dealing with the Gentiles in those days. As far as the rest of the Gentiles were concerned, God had given them up according to Romans, chapter 1, and only after the rejection of Christ on Calvary and the day of Pentecost, do we find that Gentiles are again included in the blessing of Abraham.

Today, therefore, the Church consists of both Jew and Gentile, born by the Spirit of God, and will constitute the mystery of the Bride of Christ.

191. If Adam was the first man, how do you account for the pre-historic cave man?

The Bible does not acknowledge or recognize the existence of cave men whatsoever. Science has never yet proven that there is any evidence of human life on this earth prior to Adam which we believe is about six thousand years ago. Of course, we realize that they claim a great many discoveries, and put together various bones which they claim are human bones, but there is no absolute scientific evidence of any kind to substantiate their theories concerning pre-historic man. As Christians we abide by the Word of God. While, of course, we know that the earth is probably billions of years old, we believe that man's sojourn on this earth dates back about six thousand years. There was a pre-historic creation but there is no record in the Bible that any human beings in the image of God existed at that time. In this connection I would like to refer you to just one Scripture in I Corinthians 15:45, where we are told:

> . . . The first man Adam was made a living soul . . .
> (I Cor. 15:45).

This definitely teaches that Adam was the first man.

192. Why did the Lord speak in parables?

You will find the answer to this plainly stated by the Lord Himself in the following passages:

> Therefore speak I to them in parables: because they seeing see not; and hearing they hear not, neither do they understand.
> And in them is fulfilled the prophecy of Esaias, which saith, By hearing ye shall hear, and shall not understand; and seeing ye shall see, and shall not perceive:
> For this people's heart is waxed gross, and their ears are dull of hearing, and their eyes they have closed; lest at any time they should see with their eyes and hear with their ears, and should understand with their heart, and should be converted, and I should heal them (Matt. 13:13-15).

> And when he was alone, they that were about him with the twelve asked of him the parable.
> And he said unto them, Unto you it is given to know the mystery of the kingdom of God: but unto them that are without, all these things are done in parables:
> That seeing they may see, and not perceive; and hearing they may hear, and not understand; lest at any time they should be converted, and their sins should be forgiven them (Mark 4:10-12).

In these passages it is very clear that parables were used to hide the truth from those whom He did not want to understand these truths. Parables, as the Lord Jesus Christ used them, were a method of speaking whereby those who did believe could see the truth, but those who did not believe would be kept from knowing the meaning of His words. It is the same thing as the MYSTERY of which Paul speaks, which was a mystery only to those who would not accept it, but was perfectly clear to those who did believe. I am sure that a careful reading of the passages that I have given will give you clearly this aspect of the truth. We must remember that our Lord knew that Israel would reject Him, and so He spoke in such a way that they would not receive Him, because He must go to the Cross of Calvary in order to become the Saviour of the world.

193. Was the Devil saved, and then lost when he fell? From this it would seem that we could be saved, and then lose our salvation.

The fact that the Devil fell and was cast out of Heaven has nothing to do with the doctrine of eternal security, since when we talk about this we are not talking about angels or devils, but we are talking about human beings who have been redeemed by the precious blood of the Lord Jesus Christ. Those who have been purchased by His own precious blood, of course, cannot be lost. This is not true of the Devil, and was not true of the angels, for they had never been redeemed at all. There is no connection whatsoever between the two.

194. I heard a protestant minister say that the virgin Mary prayed the first Christian prayer. Is there any Scriptural background for such a remark?

I had never before heard that the first Christian prayer was offered by the virgin Mary; this is entirely a new thought to me, but I do not see where it would make any particular difference. It may be true that the first prayer mentioned in the New Testament as being uttered by any individual was that of the virgin Mary, but we cannot attach any significance to that. There are many prayers mentioned in the Old Testament, and while they cannot strictly be called "Christian" they were, nevertheless prayers of faith, just as much as the words of the virgin Mary. I do not, however, believe that Mary's words were so much a prayer as a song of praise. After the angel had announced that she would give birth to the Messiah, she burst forth in great praise. Some people might want to call this a prayer, but I hardly think that this is correct.

195. Who are the Gentiles?

Concerning the origin of the Gentiles, you must realize that there is no mention of Gentiles in the Bible until after the Nation of Israel had been called out. Gentiles are merely all the nations of the world who are not descendants of Jacob and the twelve tribes of Israel. Israel is called "God's peculiar nation" and the other nations are therefore called "Gentiles." Strictly speaking, I suppose that we could call all the people (except Hebrews) Gentiles who lived from the time of Adam, although this is not applied until after Israel came out of the Land. We who are European in our origin are descendants of Japheth, the youngest son of Noah.

196. When was Satan expelled from Heaven?

We cannot fix the time of Satan's fall, but we do know the occasion (see Isaiah 14:12-17). When he fell in the beginning he was expelled from Heaven, as well as from the earth, but today he still has access into the presence of God as the prince of the power of the air, and will finally at the end of the age be cast out of the air, and out of the earth, into the Lake of Fire forever.

197. What kind of a tree was in the Garden of Eden, called "the tree of knowledge of good and evil?" Was it an apple tree?

The Bible is silent on the matter. After all it makes no difference, and discussions about it are a waste of time. (See Deut. 29:29.)

198. Why did the Devil choose such an ugly creature as a snake to tempt Eve?

The Bible does not say the serpent was an ugly reptile.

> Now the serpent was more subtil than any beast of the field which the Lord God had made (Gen. 3:1).

On the contrary, he was a beautiful, possibly the most beautiful, animal on earth. The word "subtil" in Genesis 3:1 does not denote evil, but wisdom. The word is "aruwn" denoting prudence and cunningness. The word "subtil" occurs twice more in our English Bible (II Samuel 13:3 and Proverbs 7:10) but an entirely different word is used. The serpent walked upright before the fall, because the curse was "upon thy belly shalt thou go" (Gen. 3:14) which of course means it did not do so before. The serpent evidently was the only animal with the power of speech, and is classified not with reptiles, but among the beasts and cattle (see Genesis 3:1, 14). If the serpent had not been a beautiful animal, Eve (like any other woman) would not have listened to a slimy, crawling snake.

199. Did God create weeds?

You ask a rather tricky question. It is possible that God made the plants which later turned to weeds. A weed is a plant "out of place." After the fall, God said of the earth, "thorns also and thistles shall it bring forth" (Gen. 3:18). There were no thorns and thistles before sin entered. Whether these were new plants, or existing plants perverted by the curse, we are not told.

200. Why did God create the Devil?

God did not create the Devil or Satan. In the beginning God created the angels, and placed over them a most exalted and beautiful creature called "Lucifer" or "the Shining One" (Isaiah 14:12). This angel sinned by rebelling against God, and was cast out by God and became the Devil and Satan (Isaiah 14:12-17; Ezekiel 28:12-19).

201. Recently my pet canary died, and I am heartbroken. Can you tell me if I will meet my pet again in Heaven?

I can give no better answer than that given by the late Dr. Harry A. Ironside when asked this same question. He said, "Sister, if God wants you to have your pets in Heaven, He will see to it that they are there."

202. Do we still have demon possession in this dispensation? It would seem from the terrible things we read in the newspapers that people must be possessed.

I do not believe that it is common in this country (actual demon possession) such as was so prevalent in the days of the Lord Jesus Christ. We must remember that many of these things which people do are not instigated by the Devil, but by the flesh of the depraved human heart. When we realize that the heart of man is "deceitful above all things and desperately wicked" and that "in the flesh dwelleth no good thing," we can account for many of these terrible crimes by remembering what God says about the human heart without Christ. I believe that most of these things are manifestations of the unregenerate human heart. There is a danger that we shall blame the Devil for the things we ourselves are guilty of. Read Matthew 15:19,

> For out of the heart proceed evil thoughts, murders, adulteries, fornications, thefts, false witness, blasphemies (Matt. 15:19).

It is possible there is demon possession today, and I have no doubt that on the foreign field the missionaries sometimes run into it. However, I believe that demon possession will not become prevalent again until after the Rapture of the Church, and during the great Tribulation.

203. Who is an apostate? Are they born-again believers, or those who have just professed but not possessed salvation?

I have never heard a fully satisfying definition of apostasy. However, it is my personal opinion that they are those who have merely made a profession of faith in the Lord Jesus Christ, and then later on depart from that profession and show their true colors as unregenerate sinners. There are, of course, others who teach that an apostate is one who has been born again, but then loses his salvation. This I cannot accept, and I believe that the instances in the Bible refer to PROFESSORS who are not true POSSESSORS.

204. I am interested in a study of the meaning of numbers in the Bible. Could you give me any help on this?

I would suggest that you try to get a book on the meaning of numbers in the Scriptures, or a numerical Bible. Your religious book store will have a variety of books on the subject. The usual meaning of numbers in the Bible is as follows:

No. 1. — The unity of God

No. 2. — Division
No. 3. — Completeness
No. 4. — The earth
No. 5. — The number of grace
No. 6. — The number of man
No. 7. — Perfection
No. 8. — A new beginning
No. 9. — Judgment
No. 10. — Testimony
No. 11. — Failure
No. 12. — The children of Israel

205. Where in the Bible does it tell us that we shall be punished seven times for our sins?

There is no passage in Scripture which states that we will have to be punished seven times for our sins. I think that possibly you are thinking of Leviticus 26:28, where we read concerning the Nation of Israel:

> Then I will walk contrary unto you also in fury; and I, even I, will chastise you seven times for your sins (Lev. 26:28).

In this verse the Lord says that He is going to chastise the Nation of Israel seven times for their sins. This, of course, has no application to our sins in this dispensation, but refers to the Nation of Israel who for these many centuries have been paying the awful price of rejecting their Lord, but will also after the Lord returns be restored in fellowship with Him. Possibly this is the verse that you had in mind.

206. My pastor made the statement that there were no crippled people who went out of Egypt into the

wilderness. Can you tell me where I can find this in the Bible?

Concerning the absence of crippled people going out of Egypt, I think that your pastor probably had in mind the statement in Psalm 105:37,

> . . . and there was not one feeble person among their tribes (Psalm 105:37).

207. **I have found a precious promise in Deuteronomy 31:8, but how can I be sure that God's promise to Moses in a particular sense is a promise which I too can claim? I was told that I could not take a promise which was given by God directly to one person years ago and claim it for myself. Please give me some help on this.**

I am sure that we have a right to claim these promises in the Old Testament if they in any way have application to us. While it is true that this promise was made by Moses to Joshua, if we find ourselves also in a similar circumstance, looking into an unknown future, there is nothing at all to prevent the Holy Spirit from taking those promises and making them our own. After all, "all Scripture is given by inspiration of God, and is profitable" (II Tim. 3:16). I think that there is a real danger in taking certain parts of the Bible and delegating them to certain individuals, whereas the Lord wants us to take it all. The primary interpretation may not be TO us, but I am sure there is an application FOR all of us.

208. **Do you think that a baby that is born dead has a soul?**

The Bible does not have a great deal to say regarding the condition of babies who die before or at birth. Personally, I believe that a full term, or nearly so, child which is born dead *does* have a soul, and God takes care of it in some way. However, it depends on the age of the foetus after conception. Just at what time the soul enters the unborn child is nowhere revealed. I am sure that we will have to wait until we get to Glory before we have the answer on this difficult problem.

However, I think that the Bible is absolutely clear that Jesus died for Adam's sin, and since little children who die before the age of responsibility do not have any personal sin of their own, they are all saved, and we are sure that we will meet them again in Heaven. Just what the condition will be, we do not know, but that will be one of the surprises when we meet our loved ones again.

209. Can you help me with the meaning of the word "heart" in Scripture? Does this refer to the physical heart or to the soul?

Concerning the meaning of the word "heart" as it occurs in Scripture, I feel quite confident in studying all the passages where it occurs, that as a rule the physical heart is not in view at all, but rather, the inner being and the inner self, and especially the old nature. As an illustration of this, Jeremiah 17:9 I am sure will answer the question. Here you remember the prophet says:

> The HEART is deceitful above all things, and desperately wicked: who can know it?
> I the LORD search the heart, I try the reins, even to give to every man according to his ways, and according to the fruit of his doings (Jer. 17:9, 10).

Here very definitely the Lord is talking about the nature of man and his inner being, and not the physical heart at all.

210. Do you think it is Scriptural to apply the term "reverend" to a person?

I am aware the the term "reverend" is only used of the Lord in the Scriptures, and I would much rather not use it. However, the world does not understand these things, and it is used only to indicate that one is a full-fledged preacher and has completed his training and has been ordained as a preacher. I realize that ordination of man means absolutely nothing, but we do have to meet certain conditions here in this world in order to do our best work for Him. Paul said:

> . . . I am made all things to all men, that I might by all means save some (I Cor. 9:22).

This is the only reason that we have stooped to use the term "reverend" which is so common in the religious circles today. I am thoroughly familiar with the evil of Nicolaitanism, and that there is no such thing as a special class of clergy found in the Scriptures, but we must beware also of a holier-than-thou spirit of criticism.

211. I would like to ask a question about losing one's salvation. The children of Israel were a type of the believer. They were saved from Egypt by the blood and were on their way to Canaan. But many of them never reached there, but after a time in the wilderness longed again for the things of Egypt and never reached the Land of Canaan.

The Israelites as a nation are a type of the believers—all saved by the blood, never to go back again to Egypt. Egypt is the picture of the bondage of sin. Canaan is the picture of VICTORY—NOT Heaven! Those who died in the wilderness were still saved from Egypt, but came short of the reward of victory. So too, believers today who fail in their wilderness journey are NOT LOST AGAIN, but come short of victory, and will suffer loss at the Judgment Seat of Christ, according to I Corinthians 3:15,

> If any man's work shall be burned, he shall suffer loss: but he himself shall be saved; yet so as by fire (I Cor. 3:15).

212. I heard a minister say that God did not have hands or feet. This is the second time I heard that said, but I still don't believe it, as I read many places in the Bible where it tells of God's hands. Do you believe that God has hands?

We must realize that God is not a man, but is a spiritual being. However, the Bible does speak of the hands and the ears and the eyes and the feet of God. This does not mean material, physical hands like we have, but it rather represents the functions which these organs usually perform in our bodies. The Lord uses these terms, "hands and feet and eyes and ears" so that we may understand something of His working and His power. God is a Spirit, and has spiritual hands. The Bible certainly does speak about the hands of God:

> Behold, the LORD's hand is not shortened, that it cannot save; neither his ear heavy, that it cannot hear (Isa. 59:1).

213. Is the word "Easter" found in Scripture?

The word "Easter" itself occurs only once in our English Bible, and then it is a mistranslation.

> And when he had apprehended him, he put him in prison, and delivered him to four quaternions of soldiers to keep him; intending after Easter to bring him forth to the people (Acts 12:4).

The word is "pascha" in the original and is a Hebrew word for "passover." The word "Easter" itself, therefore, never occurs in the Bible, but is a wrong translation, and should be changed to "passover." There is no record in the Bible that the apostles ever observed Easter. As we know, Easter was a pagan holiday dedicated to a pagan goddess, and was carried over by the Roman Catholic Church into the Christian tradition. I therefore very seldom use the word "Easter" except where it is necessary in order to make people understand to what I am referring.

214. What is the "leviathan" mentioned in Scripture?

The leviathan mentioned in Job and the Psalms and also in Isaiah is not easy to identify. The meaning of this word is not at all clear, and there is a great deal of difference of opinion among Bible students. Some think it refers to a large serpent, while others think that it has reference to a crocodile, and some others translate it as "dragon." It is one of those things that we do not know about, and will have to wait until we have more light, before we can talk about it intelligently. It is one of the secret things of the Lord with which I do not think we ought to bother.

215. What is the meaning of the word "day" as used in Scripture?

The word "day," as used in the Bible, does not always refer to the same period of time. I believe the word DAY as used in Genesis, chapter 1, means a period of twenty-four hours as it is limited to evening and morning. However, there are other "days" in Scripture such as the "Day of the Lord," which we believe will be seven years, between the Rapture and the Second Coming of Christ. Then also we read about the "Day of God" which will be the end of the world.

We oftentimes speak of "the day of judgment" which does not necessarily have to be a single day. We therefore have to read the context very carefully, and find out what the Holy Spirit is talking about before we determine the length of a day. We figure days, of course, in hours and minutes, while the Word tells us "that with the Lord a thousand years is as one day, and a day as a thousand years" (II Peter 3:8). It is not always easy to determine which is meant, but I believe that if we study it carefully, the Spirit will indicate the proper meaning.

I would pay no attention, however, to those teachers who try to make all sorts of foolish interpretations about these days. A great deal of date setting has resulted from an effort to twist the Scriptures in making them mean something different from that which it does mean.

216. Who helped God in creation? Someone told me that Lucifer had a part in it.

The entire Trinity—Father, Son, and Holy Spirit— were all operative in the creation in the beginning. In the first few verses of Genesis 1 we read that the Spirit of God moved upon the waters. This is the part of the Spirit's work. Then the Father spoke, and it was through the Word that the worlds were created. Now, of course, the Word of God is none other than the Lord Jesus Christ. He is the Creator of the worlds. In John, chapter 1, we read:

> All things were made by him, and without him was not any thing made that was made (John 1:3).

There is nothing in the Bible at all about Lucifer helping God with creation. According to Job we believe that the angels were present at the creation of the earth, but they had nothing to do with it at all. They themselves are creatures, so you may rest assured that only God is the Creator; and especially through His Son, the Lord Jesus Christ, were the worlds created.

217. Is the earth six thousand years old, or is there proof from the Bible of pre-historic life on this earth?

I am quite convinced that the creation of the earth itself took place much longer than six thousand years ago. I believe that the first verse of Genesis 1 records the creation of the original earth. This may be many millions, even billions of years ago. Then something happened which caused the earth to become in the condition which we find it in the second verse—void and formless and with darkness upon the deep. We know that God did not make the earth in this condition in the beginning, and so something must have happened. This probably occurred when Satan and his angels fell. Then in Genesis 1:2 God began the present re-creation which we believe was about six thousand years ago. Man's existence upon this earth cannot be traced back further than six thousand years, but the original creation could have been any point of time prior to this, without any conflict to Scripture at all. A few passages of Scripture that might be helpful in this connection you will find in Isaiah 14:9-14; Isaiah 24:1; Isaiah 45:18; Jeremiah 4:23-26; and Ezekiel 28:12-15.

218. What became of the Ark of the Covenant which was in the Tabernacle?

The Bible mentions the place of the Ark today. It seems quite certain that according to Revelation 11:19 it was caught up into Heaven, and is there today.

> And the temple of God was opened in heaven, and there was seen in his temple the ark of his testament: and there

were lightnings, and voices, and thunderings, and an earth-
quake, and great hail (Rev. 11:19).

The Bible does not record when it was removed, nor
how, but we have every reason to believe from the reference in this passage that at some time during the history
of Israel it was taken into Heaven and we shall find it
there when we meet the Lord.

**219. Someone told me that there is a verse in the Bible that
says there will be as many on the Lord's side as Satan
has on his. Can you tell me where I can find this
statement?**

Concerning the fact that the Lord will have as many
in number as Satan, I do not know of any Scripture in
the Bible which makes this statement at all. I imagine
that the person had in mind this verse in Matthew:

> And think not to say within yourselves, We have Abraham
> to our father: for I say unto you, that God is able of these
> stones to raise up children unto Abraham (Matt. 3:9).

I do not believe that this teaches that the Lord will
have as many as Satan.

**220. Someone told me it was not Scriptural to sing the
chorus, "Every Promise in the Book is Mine," because
all of the promises in the Bible are not for us. Is this
correct?**

I do not see any particular harm in singing the chorus,
"Every Promise in the Book is Mine." It may not be
absolutely and entirely and one hundred percent Scriptural, but I think that the general thought is that the
promises of God are for God's people, and we ought to
trust them. I do not believe that we ought to split hairs
about these little matters, but make some concessions
and accommodations. While we do not believe in tamper-

ing with the Word of God, we must also recognize that
the hymns and choruses which were written by men were
not necessarily inspired and therefore were not infallible.
We can take almost any of the songs and hymns which
we use in our churches and find something wrong with
them. Of course, I realize that the promises made to
Israel cannot all be literally applied to the Church, but
by application they can be applied to Christians, even
though the primary interpretation may be for Israel.

**221. A pastor made the statement at the funeral of a
loved one who had gone to be with the Lord, that
this one was in Heaven still interceding for us who
are left behind. To me this sounds like a Catholic
teaching, and I can think of no Scripture to support
it. Can you help me?**

There is no direct statement in the Bible whatsoever
to substantiate the teaching that our loved ones are
interceding for us in Heaven. This "smacks" to me of
Catholicism, and I do not know of any Scripture on
which it can be based.

**222. In the Tabernacle worship, where were the people
while sacrifice was made and the priests ate the shewbread?**

As to where the people were while sacrifice was made
and the priests ate the shewbread, we must remember
that this was all typical under the Old Testament. The
priest, of course, pictured the Lord Jesus Christ in His
sacrificial work, and the people stood outside; and when
the priest went in, he went representing the people.
While the people themselves did not enter the Tabernacle, they were represented by the priest, just as Christ
in Heaven today is representing us. While we are still

here upon the earth, we are already seated in heavenly places in Christ, as though we were already there. Of course, since the death and resurrection of Christ, we ourselves are priests, and we therefore have access to the very presence of God through the Lord Jesus Christ, our High Priest.

223. **Can people do the works of Satan in the name of the Lord? I know of a minister who sincerely believes what he is doing is a gift from God, but if what he is doing against the Lord's will, it must be Satan's, and he has been deceived by Satan, but HOW and WHY is what I cannot understand.**

I can do no better than to refer you to a passage of Scripture which the Lord Himself used and which I believe will answer the question better than anything I can say. I suggest that you read carefully Matthew 7:21-23.

> Not every one that saith unto me, Lord, Lord, shall enter into the kingdom of heaven: but he that doeth the will of my Father which is in heaven.
>
> Many will say to me in that day, Lord, Lord, Have we not prophesied in thy name? and in thy name have cast out devils? and in thy name done many wonderful works?
>
> And then will I profess unto them, I never knew you: depart from me, ye that work iniquity (Matt. 7:21-23).

I realize that this is a startling passage, but it is the Word of God, and certainly brings us face to face with the possibility of people preaching the Gospel and even doing miracles and wonders, and still not having the approval of God.

224. **I was told by a devout Christian that he believes sometimes we are placed in a position by the Devil where we can't do anything, nor can God do any-**

thing. My faith in God is that he can do everything or anything at any time He wants to. Am I right or wrong about this?

There is no doubt that God sometimes does permit us to be tested through the instrumentality of Satan (Job, for instance), but He always holds His hand upon our life, and will not allow us to be tempted above that which we are able to bear. There is no question that God permits the Devil to do some things, but God is still sovereign and will never permit him to go beyond what He purposes for us in our lives. Read Job 1:8-12.

> And the LORD said unto Satan, Hast thou considered my servant Job, that there is none like him in the earth, a perfect and an upright man, one that feareth God, and escheweth evil?
>
> Then Satan answered the LORD, and said, Doth Job fear God for nought?
>
> Hast not thou made an hedge about him, and about his house, and about all that he hath on every side? thou hast blessed the work of his hands, and his substance is increased in the land.
>
> But put forth thine hand now, and touch all that he hath, and he will curse thee to thy face.
>
> And the LORD said unto Satan, Behold, all that he hath is in thy power; only upon himself put not forth thine hand. So Satan went forth from the presence of the LORD (Job 1:8-12).

225. What is the meaning of the word "carnal" as applied to a person?

Concerning the natural man, the carnal man, and the spiritual man, we believe that all unconverted people are "natural" men; that is, they have only the nature of father Adam. However, we do believe that when people are saved, they have two distinct possibilities, the one being carnality, and the other being spirituality.

The carnal Christian is one who is not completely separated and dedicated unto the service of the Lord, and is still following many of the inclinations of the flesh. Paul calls the Corinthian Christians "carnal" as babes in Christ. They were definitely saved, as you can see from the introduction where he calls them "sanctified in Christ" and "saints" (I Cor. 1:2). However, they were still far from being what God would have them to be, and therefore they were called "carnal." A spiritual Christian is one who has reached spiritual maturity through the study of God's Word and obedience to His will.

226. I have friends who insist that God is the Father of all, and all men are our brothers. Is the teaching of the universal Fatherhood of God and the universal brotherhood of man Scriptural?

The teaching that God is the Father of all men is a modernistic doctrine and has absolutely no basis at all in the Scriptures. It is true, of course, that as far as our first birth is concerned, we are all children of Adam, and as such natural brothers, but only those who have been born again can call God their "Father." Jesus tells us very definitely in John 8:44 that the unconverted are the children of the Devil, and certainly are not children of God.

> Ye are of your father the devil, and the lusts of your father ye will do (John 8:44).

Those who teach the universal Fatherhood of God and the universal brotherhood of man are usually modernists who also deny the other important doctrines of the Bible. If we only stick to the Word, we will have no difficulty.

227. How many sabbaths are mentioned in the Bible, and for what purpose were they made?

All of the feast days mentioned in Leviticus 23 were sabbath days. Then, too, the seventh year was called a "sabbatic year" in the Scriptures. In addition to this, of course, we have the Old Testament seventh-day sabbath. We must be very careful that we do not confuse the ceremonial sabbaths, and think that they all apply to the seventh day of the week.

Generally speaking there are at least eight sabbath days which are so called, and, in addition, the seventh year which is called the "sabbatic year." Then, too, the fiftieth year is usually considered the year of jubilee and corresponds to a sabbatic year.

228. What is your reaction to "Sputnik"?

I believe that this is a repetition of the eleventh chapter of Genesis, where Nimrod sought to explore the heavens in the tower of Babel. We seem to be in the same rut again, and as it then was ended by the coming down of the Lord, I believe that the result is going to be the same. Let us keep looking up, for one of these days it will really happen, and the Lord will return!

229. What books do you find most helpful in your preparation of messages?

I find that in the preparation of my messages the most valuable books which I possess are a *Scofield Reference Bible,* a copy of Scofield's *Rightly Dividing the Word of Truth, Strong's Concordance,* and the *Davis Bible Dictionary.* I believe that these four books are more valuable in studying the Word of God than probably any other. In addition to this, I use freely the *International Bible Encyclopedia,* and I am also familiar with the Holland and German languages which I find to be very helpful in my study of the Word. Hebrew and Greek lexicons are valuable, but if you are not familiar with the Greek and Hebrew grammar, it would be of little use to you.

230. Do animals have souls?

We must not confuse the SOUL of an animal with the SPIRIT of man. Man consists of a body, a soul, and a spirit, the spirit being that part which makes him able to fellowship with God in spiritual things. However, an animal has a soul in the sense that it has physical life, but it has no spiritual perception, no sense of sin, and of course, no consciousness of God. Only in this sense are animals said to have souls.

231. Does a dog have a soul, and when it dies where does it go?

Dogs, like other animals, have a soul but the Bible does not tell us that animals have an immortal soul; when they die they perish, and will never be resurrected again. As to where they go when they die, they simply cease to exist. Nowhere in the Bible does it say that they have a responsible soul, or will live again.

232. A friend of mine believes that all animals have a soul and will be redeemed and uses Romans 8:19-22 for the Scripture. He also says that if a person kills an animal, it is considered murder, and will have to be accounted for before God. Will you please give me your belief on this.

We believe that man was created in the image of God, and therefore has eternal existence. However, the animal creation was not created in the image of God, and there-

fore does not have a spirit and a soul such as man has.
When an animal dies, it ceases to exist. It goes back to
the earth, and that is the end. There will be no resurrection of animals.

In regard to the redemption of creation (Romans
8:19-22), every realm of creation which came under
Adam's curse will be redeemed, but this does not mean
that each and every animal that ever lived will share
in this redemption. This is a redemption of creation as
a whole, rather than as an individual redemption for
animals.

The Bible nowhere states that it is a sin to kill an
animal. In the Old Testament the children of Israel
were allowed and permitted to eat all manner of clean
foods, and in the New Testament also it is definitely
stated that we are to call nothing common or unclean.
The only restriction is that we are not to eat the blood
of anything which has been strangled, so that the blood
has remained in the carcass. If the Bible prohibited the
killing of any kind of life, we could not kill flies or poison
potato bugs, or spray for any kind of insects whatsoever.
This is entirely absurd, and there is absolutely nothing
in the Bible at all which says it is a sin to kill an animal.
Of course, if we torture animals, that becomes a sin,
but not in the ordinary course of providing for food or
of making our living.

233. What do you think about women preachers, and do you think they should be ordained to the ministry?

I personally believe that there is a place for women
to teach, and to be used of the Lord in many ways, but
I do not believe that a woman is to be the head of a

church or the pastor of an organization without being under the direction of the man. I believe that this is the order of the Lord. I certainly do not believe that a woman must be put in a corner, and not allowed to speak at all, but everything she does must be under the direction and supervision of the man who is the head, under Christ, and then we know that the blessing of the Lord can rest upon it.

I do not believe that the Bible anywhere teaches that women should take the place of authority in the Church in teaching or in preaching. I therefore do not believe that there is any precedent in the Bible for ordaining women to preach. There is not one verse in Scripture to give any support to this. It is entirely a manmade institution.

234. Will we know our loved ones in Heaven?

The Bible, I believe, is very clear that we shall know our loved ones when we get to Heaven. The disciples of the Lord recognized Him after His resurrection. Then too, the Bible tells us in Matthew 17 that the disciples on the Mount of Transfiguration readily recognized both Moses and Elijah, although they had never seen them before. In Luke 16 even the rich man in *Hades* recognized both Lazarus, and Abraham in whose bosom he was reposing.

In I Thessalonians 4 we are told that we "shall be caught up TOGETHER," and that implies that we shall recognize one another. Also in I Corinthians 13 we are distinctly told that "we shall know even as also we are known." There can be no question that we will know one another in Heaven, although it will be in quite a different way than here upon this sinful earth.

235. Where is Hell located? I heard a preacher say it is in the center of the earth.

The Bible does not locate Hell (the Lake of Fire). It is called "outer darkness" (Matthew 8:12), and a place where the "worm dieth not, and the fire is not quenched" (Mark 9:44). It is a place "prepared for the devil and his angels" (Matthew 25:41).

However, Hades ("sheol" in the Old Testament) is located in the heart of the earth. This is the temporary abode of the souls of men after death. There are only lost souls in Hades now. These will be cast into Hell at the end of the ages (Revelation 20:11-15).

236. Recently an evangelist in our community made the statement that "the opinion of many was that there would be no tears in Heaven." He said that this was false; that there would be tears in Heaven. Please explain this to me.

Concerning "tears in Heaven," we must make a sharp distinction between the Judgment Seat of Christ which will be before the Millennium, and the eternal state. We believe that in eternity, after the Millennium, there will be no tears, but I am sure that there will be many tears at the Judgment Seat of Christ, and regrets during the Kingdom Age for opportunities which have been lost.

237. I am wondering in the parable of the sower, if there weren't two saved represented in this group. This is hard for me to comprehend, as one of these that is supposed to be unsaved "believed for a while."

There is a great difference of opinion among good Bible students as to the exact interpretation of the last three cases of the seed which fell on stony ground, among thorns, and on good ground. Of course, there is no question about the last, which brought forth fruit, thirty, sixty, and an hundredfold. In regard to the first, there is also no question, since it never did produce anything, but was immediately picked up by the enemy.

While I would not be dogmatic in any way, I believe that which fell upon stony ground represents those who only have an intellectual acceptance and an emotional response to the message when they hear it, but it never comes to any fruitage whatsoever. I believe that they represent those who have had only an emotional experience, but never have believed in their hearts.

In regard to those who fell among the thorns, my belief has always been that they may represent Christians who do not go on to fruitbearing. They are probably those who will lose their reward at the Judgment Seat of Christ.

While this is my personal opinion, I do not hold myself up as an authority, and some day when we get to Glory we will understand all of these things. There are good men who sincerely hold that only the ones who fell upon good ground were really saved.

238. I have listened to your broadcast for many years, and one thing bothers me. I would say that ninety-nine percent of the time you close your prayer with the words, "in Jesus' name," and I would prefer that you use the full name, "The Lord Jesus Christ."

I have considered your kindly criticism of the use of the name *Jesus,* and not always using the full name *the Lord Jesus Christ* as frequently as you think it appropriate and fitting, but I personally see no harm in using the name JESUS by itself.

If you will refer to your concordance, you will find that in the New Testament the name JESUS by itself alone is used four times oftener than the full name, *the Lord Jesus Christ*. The name JESUS by itself is used one hundred and thirty times, while the words *Lord Jesus Christ* are used less than forty times.

Also, may I kindly remind you that you are entirely incorrect in saying that ninety-nine percent of the time I end my prayer, "in Jesus' Name." This is grossly exaggerated, but I gladly forgive you.

I trust you will go through the uses of the name JESUS in the New Testament, and see how often it is used alone. See Matthew 1:21, 25; 4:1, 17; 8:3, 10; 12:25; Luke 1:31; 2:21; etc.

239. Please explain to me why Israel is referred to in the masculine gender. We always use the feminine gender in our language in referring to a country.

Concerning the reason why ISRAEL is spoken of in the masculine gender, you must remember that the Israelites are the descendants of the twelve SONS of Jacob, and the Nation is also called by God "His son" (Hosea 11:1). Israel nationally is referred to as a son also (see Exodus 4:22).

CHAPTER XIII

PROBLEMS AND PERPLEXITIES
ON PUZZLING PASSAGES
(Part I — Old Testament)

240. In Genesis 2:7 can the word "spirit" be substituted for "breath of life"?

> And the LORD God formed man of the dust of the ground, and breathed into his nostrils the breath of life; and man became a living soul (Gen. 2:7).

Concerning this verse and the advisability of substituting the word SPIRIT for BREATH OF LIFE, I do not see any reason for doing so, although I do not believe it would change the meaning in any sense whatsoever. The word translated "spirit" in the Old Testament is the same word which is also translated "wind," and therefore may be used to mean "breath of life." I do not believe that there would be anything wrong in substituting the word, as the meaning would not be essentially changed.

241. In Genesis, chapter 5, while there are six "and He died" before Enoch's translation, what do you do with two more of the same "and He died" AFTER Enoch was translated?

The six generations of death preceding the rapture of Enoch are a clear picture of the six ages of man's

157

bungling, to be followed by the Rapture and the age of millennial peace. Of course, the fact that death still occurred after Enoch's rapture is in perfect harmony with the fact that even during the millenial period when Christ reigns, there will still be death upon the earth, although it will be the rare exception. Not until the new heavens and the new earth are created will death be entirely put away.

242. How do you reconcile Matthew 22:30 and Mark 12:25 with Genesis 6? If angels are sexless, how could they be the parents of the monstrosities mentioned in Genesis 6?

Matthew 22:30 reads as follows:

> For in the resurrection they neither marry, nor are given in marriage, but are as the angels of God in heaven (Matt. 22:30).

In Mark 12:25 we read:

> For when they shall rise from the dead, they neither marry, nor are given in marriage; but are as the angels which are in heaven (Mark 12:25).

Concerning these passages, and the angels being sexless, you must remember that in this passage the Lord is speaking about angels IN HEAVEN. He is not here referring to the fallen angels which we believe are mentioned in Genesis 6. It was the sin of these fallen angels, that they produced this unholy union in the days of Noah, but the Lord Jesus said when He was here on earth, "IN HEAVEN they neither marry nor are given in marriage." However, angels are always spoken of in the masculine. There are no female angels and, of course, no baby angels. The Bible does not say angels are "sexless" but simply that they do not marry. In Genesis 6 it was illicit co-habitation of demons (not holy angels) and humans.

243. I heard you state that the "sons of God" in Genesis 6 were angels. We just cannot go along with that according to our Bible. Angels are sexless and are "not given in marriage." We would rather believe that the "sons of God" were of the line of Seth. We would certainly appreciate an answer, as this has been a great controversy in our circles.

Concerning the angels called the "sons of God" in Genesis 6, you are quite mistaken when you say that "angels are sexless beings." There is not a verse in the Bible that says that angels do not have sex. In fact, angels are always spoken of in the masculine gender. I infer that you probably base your conclusion on the passage in Matthew 22, verse 30, where the Lord Jesus says:

> For in the resurrection they neither marry, nor are given in marriage, but are as the angels of God in heaven (Matt. 22:30).

Will you please notice that in this verse the Lord Jesus is NOT speaking about fallen angels, but is speaking about UNFALLEN ANGELS OF GOD IN HEAVEN. If the sons of God in Genesis 6 were the children of Seth, then we can still not account for the fact that they became giants and monstrosities, since it is not true physically, that the offspring of mixed marriages necessarily are physical giants or monstrous beings.

However, it need not be a matter of big controversy, since every one is entitled to his own personal opinion. I believe that we ought to hold our own opinion on these matters in perfect charity and love toward one another, and never make it the basis of an argument. Some day we shall know and understand all these things fully.

244. Who are the "sons of God" mentioned in Genesis 6 who married the "daughters of men"?

Some say the "sons of God" were the descendants of Seth, who married the daughters of Cain. However, this would imply that all Seth's children were boys and all Cain's children were girls. Moreover, it would infer all Seth's children were believers and all Cain's were unbelievers. But even if this were true, this would not account for their offspring being giants. The children are not affected PHYSICALLY by the faith of their parents.

Rather, we believe the "sons of God" were fallen angels, who cohabited with human women, in an effort to corrupt the race and so prevent the coming of the promised "human seed." Fallen angels are called "sons of God" (Job 1:6; Job 2:1).

> Now there was a day when the SONS OF GOD came to present themselves before the LORD, and Satan came also among them (Job 1:6).
>
> Again there was a day when the SONS OF GOD came to present themselves before the LORD, and Satan came also among them to present himself before the LORD (Job 2:1).

They are undoubtedly the same as the wicked angels of Jude 6:

> And the angels which kept not their first estate, but left their own habitation, he hath reserved in everlasting chains under darkness unto the judgment of the great day (Jude 6).

The result was giants (fallen ones—the word is "nephilim"). Only Noah's family was untainted (Gen. 6:9) and perfect in his "generations." To prevent the total corruption of humanity, God sent the flood.

245. Where in the Bible besides Genesis 9, are the colored race mentioned?

The colored people are the descendants of Noah's son, Ham. However, the colored people are not mentioned as such in Genesis 9. The colored people are the descendants of Ham and of Canaan, in the 9th chapter of Genesis, but they were not colored people at that time. However, they are mentioned several times throughout the Scriptures, and are referred to as Ethiopians rather than colored people. You will find Ethiopians mentioned in Numbers 12:1; Jeremiah 38:7; and also in Acts 8:27.

The color of their skin is the genetic result of generations of exposure to intense sunlight. A sun-tan is an example.

246. How do you reconcile Genesis 32:30 with Exodus 33:20?

> And Jacob called the name of the place Peniel: for I have seen God face to face, and my life is preserved (Gen. 32:30).
>
> And he said, Thou canst not see my face: for there shall no man see me, and live (Ex. 33:20).

In regard to the "apparent" discrepancy in Genesis 32:30 and Exodus 33:20, we must remember that it is all explained by the words of our Lord Jesus Christ in the New Testament, when He says:

> No man hath seen God at any time; the only begotten Son, which is in the bosom of the Father, he hath declared him (John 1:18).

It is very evident, therefore, that in Exodus 33:20 it was God the Father whom Moses COULD NOT SEE; while in Genesis 32:30 it was the appearance of the Second Person of the Trinity, the Lord Jesus Christ, whom Jacob saw. In this way there is no contradiction.

247. Concerning Exodus 4:24-26, why did the Lord seek to kill Moses?

> And it came to pass by the way in the inn, that the LORD met him, and sought to kill him.
>
> Then Zipporah took a sharp stone, and cut off the foreskin of her son, and cast it at his feet, and said, Surely a bloody husband art thou to me.
>
> So he let him go: then she said, A bloody husband thou art, because of the circumcision (Ex. 4:24-26).

The reason for the attempt of the Lord to kill Moses was because Moses had neglected the circumcision of his son while in Egypt. After his son was circumcised by Moses' wife, the wrath of the Lord was appeased, and the Lord did not slay him.

248. I am troubled concerning the verses in Exodus 8:15; 9:7; and 9:12. What does it mean in these verses about God "hardening Pharaoh's heart"?

> But when Pharaoh saw that there was respite, HE HARD-ENED HIS HEART, and hearkened not unto them; as the LORD had said (Ex. 8:15).
>
> And Pharaoh sent, and, behold, there was not one of the cattle of the Israelites dead. And the HEART OF PHARAOH WAS HARDENED, and he did not let the people go (Ex. 9:7).
>
> And the LORD HARDENED THE HEART of Pharaoh, and he hearkened not unto them; as the LORD had spoken unto Moses (Ex. 9:12).

Concerning the hardening of Pharaoh's heart, there are two things which must be remembered. First of all, it must be read in the light of Romans 9:17, where it is definitely said that God raised up Pharaoh for the very purpose of which the Book of Exodus tells us:

> For the scripture saith unto Pharaoh, Even for this same purpose have I raised thee up, that I might shew my power

in thee, and that my name might be declared throughout all the earth (Rom. 9:17).

This, of course, refers to the sovereignty of God.

On the other hand, we must remember that in the Book of Exodus we have at least three different stages in the hardening of Pharaoh's heart. We read in Exodus 8:15 that Pharaoh "hardened his heart." In Exodus 9:7 we have the record, "and the heart of Pharaoh was hardened," and in Exodus 9:12 we have the record, "and the Lord hardened the heart of Pharaoh." I believe that we have to look at it in two ways. God did in sovereign power harden the heart of Pharaoh; but as far as Pharaoh was concerned, he *first* hardened his heart, and then his heart was hardened; and, finally, God completed the process. I hope that this answers your question.

249. In Exodus 29:20 what is the significance of the blood on the tip of the ear, right thumb, and big toe?

Then shalt thou kill the ram, and take of his blood, and put it upon the tip of the RIGHT EAR of Aaron, and upon the tip of the RIGHT EAR of his sons, and upon the THUMB OF THEIR RIGHT HAND, and upon the GREAT TOE OF THEIR RIGHT FOOT, and sprinkle the blood upon the altar round about (Ex. 29:20).

The blood on the right ear, thumb of the right hand, and big toe of the right foot of the priest signifies that his entire service is dedicated unto the Lord. The blood on the ear, together with the oil, indicates that he is dedicated to "hearing" the voice of the Lord and obeying it. The right thumb, as the principal digit of the hand, speaks of "service," and indicates that the priest is now consecrated to full service of the Lord; while the blood on the right toe speaks of his "walk" and his conduct in the world. All of this, of course, is typical and teaches us that we too are to dedicate our ears, hands, and feet—in fact, our whole being—to the service of the Lord.

250. I have a problem concerning the passage in Exodus 32:32, 33. Is a person's name after being saved written in GOD'S BOOK, or the BOOK OF LIFE mentioned in Revelation 20:15, and could it be blotted out by sinning?

> Yet now, if thou wilt forgive their sin—; and if not, blot me, I pray thee, out of thy book which thou hast written.
> And the LORD said unto Moses, Whosoever hath sinned against me, him will I blot out of my book (Ex. 32:32, 33).

Let me say, first of all, that this is a rather obscure passage and has given Bible students difficulty, and as a result there are three main schools of thought regarding its meaning. They are:

1. The names of all are recorded in the Book of Life at birth, and then when a person sins or rejects the way of salvation, his name is removed from the Book.

2. Others say that the names are placed in the Book of Life when a person is saved, and that if they sin and go back into the old life, then their names are removed.

3. Perhaps the most satisfying interpretation is that this blotting the name out of the Book does not refer to the loss of salvation, but rather to the loss of rewards.

For the full answer we shall have to wait until we get to Heaven.

251. Please explain Exodus 34 in the light of Deuteronomy 10.

Concerning the seeming contradictions between the giving of the Law in Exodus 34 and Deuteronomy 10, I think that the order of events is as follows:

First, Moses received the tables of the law from the

Lord, written by the finger of God. These tables were broken at the foot of the mountain when he returned from the top of the mountain.

Then the Lord commanded him to bring up two tables of stone upon which the Lord was to write the second edition of the commandments. These second tables of the law were then placed within a wooden box, or an ark, which Moses took with him when he went into the mountain to receive the second tables. This ark is described in Deuteronomy 10:1-5. Evidently this law was to be kept in the wooden box or ark, and was never to be looked at.

In regard to the writing which Moses did, there are two views:

1. One states that Moses made a complete copy of the original law which was to be placed on display for the children of Israel. The first tables were broken, and the second ones which were rewritten were to be hid in the ark of the covenant.

2. The other view holds that God wrote the Ten Commandments upon the Tables of Stone both times, while Moses wrote all the other precepts and laws and regulations concerning hygiene, government, etc., contained in the books of Exodus, Leviticus, and Deuteronomy.

These things are sometimes difficult to understand, but as you say in your letter, there can be no contradiction. Personally, I believe that God wrote the first tables of the law which were broken, and also wrote upon the second tables, and that Moses was the one who was to write all the rest of the laws and regulations which were not included in the Ten Commandments.

252. Please explain "the sins of the parents shall fall on their children" as stated in Exodus 34:7 and Numbers 14:18. Why must children suffer for the sins of others?

> . . . visiting the iniquity of the fathers upon the children, and upon the children's children, unto the third and to the fourth generation (Ex. 34:7).

> The LORD is longsuffering, and of great mercy, forgiving iniquity and transgression, and by no means clearing the guilty, visiting the iniquity of the fathers upon the children unto the third and fourth generation (Num. 14:18).

We must face the facts—even though we cannot always explain them. It is not something that we must understand, but something that we have to believe, because it is definitely taught in the Word of God. We know that all the trouble and difficulty and sorrow in the world today is because of Adam's sin, and this alone proves that God does visit the sins of the fathers upon the children. No other satisfactory answer has ever been advanced for the existence of suffering and death.

Then, too, we know that children suffer because of what parents do. Parents transmit not only their nature, but often disease to their offspring, in which they have had no part whatsoever. This is not a matter to be denied or questioned, but simply a matter we have to recognize and face because it happens to be a fact.

253. In Numbers 19:2, why was the red heifer picked as a sacrifice?

> This is the ordinance of the law which the LORD hath commanded, saying, Speak unto the children of Israel, that they bring thee a RED HEIFER without spot, wherein is no blemish, and upon which never came yoke (Num. 19:2).

This was one of the sacrifices which pointed forward

especially to the high priestly and cleansing work of the Lord Jesus Christ. While the sacrifice of the lamb and the bullock upon the altar of burnt-offering typified our justification through the sacrifice of Christ, it is the RED HEIFER particularly which speaks of the cleansing of the believer after he has been saved. It is again through the blood of the Lord Jesus Christ, so that the red heifer had to be sacrificed. The sevenfold sprinkling of the blood is the completion and the perfection of His work which He does for us in making us like Himself. The reduction of the sacrifice to complete ashes is a reminder that all of our own righteousness is absolutely worthless, and we must depend entirely upon the death of another. When the ashes are added to the water, it speaks of the work of the Holy Spirit, and the Word. As you undoubtedly know, the water symbolizes both the WORD OF GOD and the SPIRIT OF GOD; and thus the cleansing work, through confession of the Lord Jesus Christ, is applied to our hearts through the promise of the Word, "If we confess our sins, he is faithful and just to forgive us our sins, and to cleanse us from all unrighteousness" (I John 1:9). I believe this to be the meaning of the ordinance of the "red heifer."

254. **In my Bible reading I came across the verse in Deuteronomy 14:26. According to this it seems that permission is given to spend money for strong drink, etc. I need some help on understanding this particular passage.**

And thou shalt bestow that money for whatsoever thy soul lusteth after, for oxen, or for sheep, or for wine, or for strong drink, or for whatsoever thy soul desireth: and thou shalt eat there before the LORD thy God, and thou shalt rejoice, thou and thine household (Deut. 14:26).

It is true that according to the law which Moses gave
to the children of Israel they were allowed to celebrate
on this particular occasion by the purchasing of wine
and also strong drink. Why this was allowed I do not
know. It is, of course, clear to you that in the Bible the
USE of wine is not so much forbidden, as the ABUSE of
it. Throughout the Scriptures, wine speaks of joy, and
while it would be hard to prove that the Bible, especially
the Old Testament, forbids its use for any occasion, there
is absolutely nothing in the Scripture which justifies or
ever encourages the excessive use or the abuse of it.

Although we must admit that Deuteronomy 14:26
does permit the use of these things, it certainly is not an
argument for the use of liquor. These are some of the
things that we may not understand now, but when we
see Him face to face we shall have perfect knowledge,
and understand all things.

255. What is meant by "dogs" mentioned in Deuteronomy 23:18?

> Thou shalt not bring the hire of a whore, or the price of
> a dog, into the house of the LORD thy God for any vow: for
> even both these are abomination unto the LORD thy God
> (Deut. 23:18).

A dog was an unclean animal, and therefore was carefully avoided by the orthodox Israelite. No Bible-believing Israelite would own a dog, for they were merely
scavengers that wandered from place to place, and therefore were unclean. For this reason, the Lord would not
permit the purchase money of such an animal to be used
in the service of the Lord.

256. In reading the verse in Joshua 10:13, it seems to me as though the earth does not revolve, but the sun

revolves around the earth. What do you think about this passage, and how do you reconcile it with the teachings of science?

And the sun stood still, and the moon stayed, until the people had avenged themselves upon their enemies. Is not this written in the book of Jasher? So the sun stood still in the midst of heaven, and hasted not to go down about a whole day (Josh. 10:13).

In regard to your question concerning the sun standing still, it is an interesting fact that the Hebrew word translated "stand still" is "daman" and means literally "cease working," so that if we read this verse literally it would be "sun ceased working." Since we know that the revolution of the earth is caused by the gravitation and the pull of the sun, we have the explanation of Joshua's long day. When Joshua said the "sun ceased working" the gravitational pull of the sun was lifted, and the earth slowed up in its revolution, and hence the long day of Joshua. Instead of being a contradiction with science, it is entirely in harmony with all the known facts of nature. The Bible already taught the revolution of the earth thousands of years before science discovered it.

257. I am confused concerning the "evil spirit from the Lord" mentioned in I Samuel, chapters 16 and 18.

The question concerning the evil spirit from the Lord which came upon Saul as recorded in I Samuel, chapters 16 and 18, presents a difficulty to many; but we must remember that God is also the Lord of the spirits, and of the entire creation. While the Lord is sovereign, He permits Satan to do certain things in the accomplishment of God's plan and purpose. We must remember that God can use even the Devil and the evil spirits to carry out His designs and His plans. The expression, therefore, "an evil spirit from the Lord," does not mean that this spirit came directly from the Lord, but rather that He permitted it, and ordered it so that he was allowed to come and appear to the wicked king Saul.

258. I have a question concerning I Kings 8:9. The Tables of the Law were in the Ark, but what happened to the rod and manna?

> There was nothing in the ark save the two tables of stone, which Moses put there at Horeb, when the Lord made a covenant with the children of Israel, when they came out of the land of Egypt (I Kings 8:9).

I am afraid that I cannot give you a satisfactory answer. It is one of the things which is not revealed in the Word of God, and we will have to wait until we get to Glory to find out. What happened to the budding rod of Aaron and the golden pot of manna we do not know, except that in the Book of Revelation we are told that the hidden manna is still in existence, and undoubtedly was caught up with the Ark of the Covenant sometime during Israel's history. There is no doubt about the Ark and the manna being in Heaven, according to Revelation 2:17 and 11:19.

> . . . To him that overcometh will I give to eat of the hidden manna . . . (Rev. 2:17).
> And the temple of God was opened in heaven, and there was seen in his temple the ark of his testament . . . (Rev. 11:19).

Beyond this we cannot go.

259. I have difficulty in understanding what is meant in II Chronicles 18:22.

> Now therefore, behold, the Lord hath put a lying spirit

in the mouth of these thy prophets, and the LORD hath spoken evil against thee (II Chron. 18:22).

We must always remember that the Lord is sovereign in all of His dealings, and He has the right to blind the eyes of those whom He does not want to see the truth. We know, for instance, that Israel was blinded according to Romans 11:7, and also that God will in the future send strong delusion upon those that have not believed the truth (II Thess. 2:11, 12). In the same way the Lord allowed an evil spirit to carry out His purpose and His design in II Chronicles 18:22.

We must remember that God can even use the Devil to carry out His divine and sovereign purposes. I realize that these passages are hard to understand, as they belong to the "deep things of God," but I am sure that we must admit that God in His sovereignty has a right to do just exactly as He pleases.

260. Please explain to me the meaning of Job 38:14.

It is turned as clay to the seal; and they stand as a garment (Job 38:14).

This verse is a part of God's answer to Job. The first verse of Job 38 tells us that God answered Job out of the whirlwind, and is revealing to Job how puny and small he is in the sight of Almighty God. In the 12th verse he is speaking of the passage of time and the coming of morning and evening, and the succession of days; and the Lord asked Job whether he understood how all of this is brought about. This is the meaning of the 14th verse: "It is turned as clay to the seal; and they stand as a garment." The connection is that God is speaking about the succession of days, and the figure of clay to the seal is an ancient one. When a document was sealed, they made an impression with the signet of a ring or other

official object in wet clay, and when this wet clay dried,
it formed a seal which could not be legally broken. God
is telling Job that the days and the mornings and the
evenings are determined, and no one can break the
rule and the law of their succession, and the deeds done
cannot be undone, but are fixed as a seal.

261. Please explain to me what is meant in Psalm 8:4 by the words "man" and "son of man."

> What is man, that thou are mindful of him? and the
> son of man, that thou visitest him? (Psalm 8:4).

The reference to "man" and "son of man" in Psalm
8 refers both to MAN as a creature, and Jesus Christ as
THE SON OF MAN (see Hebrews 2:6-11). The phrase,
"that thou art mindful of him" refers to MAN (all of
us). Why God should be so mindful of us, and remember
us to save us was the object of David's amazement and
wonder.

262. Please explain what the "rod" is in Psalm 23.

> . . . thy ROD and thy staff they comfort me (Psalm 23:4).

The *rod* in Psalm 23 is a shepherd's "crook." It was
used for climbing, for counting the sheep (passing under
the rod), and for retrieving and bringing back straying
sheep by putting the crook of the rod around its neck.
It was also used to ward off the enemies of the sheep.

263. Can we take Psalm 37:25 literally?

> I have been young, and now am old; yet have I not seen
> the righteous forsaken, nor his seed begging bread (Psalm
> 37:25).

I sincerely believe that we can take this literally, and
that it had been David's experience in all of his life, that
he had never seen the "righteous forsaken, nor his seed
begging bread." This does not, of course, mean that

God's people never have any lack, but rather that they are looking to the Lord for the supply of their needs, and not to men.

I sincerely believe that if God's people would look to the Lord for the supply of their needs, instead of using carnal means and seeking human help without the Lord, that it could be said of them, "I have never seen the righteous forsaken, nor his seed begging bread." The necessity to beg bread from men is due to failure to trust and submit to God's will.

264. Concerning Psalm 90:4, it speaks of "a thousand years being as yesterday" or a day, and then it also states that it is "as a watch in the night." I would appreciate help on this.

> For a thousand years in thy sight are but as yesterday when it is past, and as a watch in the night (Psalm 90:4).

In regard to this statement, we must of course remember that God is timeless, and that time is a human concept which has been made necessary by the things which have been created. Before matter was created there was no need for time, and therefore God has no past, and He has no future, but He lives in the eternal present. The statement, therefore, in Psalm 90:4, and also in II Peter 3:8 is an accommodation to our way of thinking.

The Psalmist distinctly says that "a day in God's sight is but as yesterday when it is past," which really amounts to no time at all. The addition of the phrase, "watch in the night," again emphasizes the fact that time means nothing to the Almighty. However, in spite of the difficulty, we do believe that God's program of creation is based on the plan of a seven-day, prophetic week, and in this connection we fit in Hosea 6:1, 2:

> Come, and let us return unto the LORD: for he hath torn, and he will heal us; he hath smitten, and he will bind us up.
>
> After two days will he revive us: in the third day he will raise us up, and we shall live in his sight (Hosea 6:1, 2).

It is not necessary that we understand all of these things, but we can see the general plan and the main outline of the events as God has revealed them in His Word.

265. Is it all right for us to call our pastor "Reverend"? According to Psalm 111:9 it would seem that this title belongs only to God.

> He sent redemption unto his people: he hath commanded his covenant for ever: HOLY AND REVEREND IS HIS NAME (Psalm 111:9).

We believe that the only one who is to be called "reverend" is the Lord. By common usage, however, it is applied to ministers, and while it is not absolutely Scriptural, it is an adopted custom, and I suppose there is not much that we can do about it.

266. Please explain Psalm 126:6 to me.

> He that goeth forth and weepeth, bearing precious seed, shall doubtless come again with rejoicing, bringing his sheaves with him (Psalm 126:6).

Scripture has both a primary interpretation and secondary applications. The primary interpretation of Psalm 126:6 is undoubtedly to the Person of the Lord Jesus Christ, as all the other Scriptures are. But it also has an application to us, and we may make this application. This is true of all the Bible. It has a primary interpretation, and oftentimes many practical applications which are perfectly legitimate and can be applied unto ourselves.

Dogmatic, hair-splitting Bible teachers often forget

this principle of Bible study, and they confine themselves to the interpretation and forget the application. Then there are others who are occupied only with the applications, without any regard to the primary interpretation.

I believe that both of these must be taken into consideration, and then Psalm 126:6 applies both to the Lord Jesus Christ and to us who are admonished to go out and win souls for Him.

267. There are two passages of Scripture which seem to me a contradiction. How do we reconcile Ecclesiastes 1:4 with Revelation 21:1?

In Ecclesiastes 1:4 it states that:

> One generation passeth away and another generation cometh, but the earth abideth FOREVER.

Then in Revelation 21:1 we read:

> And I saw a new heaven and a new earth, FOR THE FIRST HEAVEN AND THE FIRST EARTH WERE PASSED AWAY. . . .

There is no contradiction between these two passages. The DESTRUCTION of the earth does not mean its ANNIHILATION. The earth will be purified by fire, but it will remain in existence, and out of it will come the NEW EARTH, in which will dwell righteousness. Therefore, the passage in Ecclesiastes merely means that the earth as a substance will abide forever, and the passage in Revelation 21 means that it will be destroyed in the sense of being re-cast, and made into a new earth.

268. In Ecclesiastes 12:7, how can the unsaved soul's spirit return to God?

> Then shall the dust return to the earth as it was: AND THE SPIRIT SHALL RETURN UNTO GOD who gave it (Eccl. 12:7).

In this verse the word "spirit" must be understood as representing the SOUL, and not the SPIRIT as we think of it in New Testament language. Read Ecclesiastes 3:21,

> Who knoweth the spirit of man that goeth upward, and the spirit of the beast that goeth downward to the earth? (Eccl. 3:21).

Here the author refers to the SPIRIT OF THE BEAST. It cannot refer to our spiritual life, but to the soul.

Moreover in Ecclesiastes 12:7 it is not said that these are the spirits of the UNSAVED, but we assume that it is those who have been redeemed. Of course, we cannot build our doctrine of the difference between soul and spirit in the Old Testament, because it is only fully revealed in the New Testament.

269. I have heard that Isaiah 7:14 cannot refer to Christ because of what is stated in the two verses which follow (Isaiah 7:15, 16). Can you please help me?

> Therefore the Lord himself shall give you a sign; Behold, a virgin shall conceive, and bear a son, and shall call his name Immanuel.
> Butter and honey shall he eat, that he may know to refuse the evil, and choose the good.
> For before the child shall know to refuse the evil, and choose the good, the land that thou abhorrest shall be forsaken of both her kings (Isa. 7:14-16).

Any one passage of the Bible must always be interpreted in the light of the entire Book. This is true in regard to your question concerning Isaiah 7:14. We should always interpret the Bible in the light of the rest of Scripture; and by turning, therefore, to Matthew 1:22, 23 we have the Holy Spirit through Matthew telling us definitely that Isaiah 7:14 refers to the Lord

Jesus Christ. By reading this passage in Matthew 1:22, 23 there is absolutely no doubt as to the meaning of that verse.

> Now all this was done, that it might be fulfilled which was spoken of the Lord by the prophet, saying,
>
> Behold, a virgin shall be with child, and shall bring forth a son, and they shall call his name EMMANUEL, which being interpreted is, God with us (Matt. 1:22, 23).

Isaiah 7:15 merely refers to the plainness of the Lord Jesus Christ in His humanity; and, of course, verse 16 has been fulfilled already and is now history. However, you must remember that the passage in Matthew gives us the Holy Spirit's interpretation, no matter what other things and difficulties may present themselves.

270. Does the 18th chapter of Isaiah have reference to the United States?

I am exceedingly sorry that it is not within the confines of a letter to give an exposition of the 18th chapter of Isaiah. However, I will say this, that I fail to see any direct reference to the United States of America in this chapter. I realize that many other Bible teachers make much of it, but I need further light before I can accept that interpretation. I believe that there are enough things clearly taught, that we do not need to be too much concerned about mere speculations.

271. Isaiah 65:20 has always been a difficult passage for me to understand. Can you give me any help on it?

> There shall be no more thence an infant of days, nor an old man that hath not filled his days: for the child shall die an hundred years old; but the sinner being an hundred years old shall be accursed (Isa. 65:20).

The reference in this verse is to the Kingdom age— the Millennium. In the Millennium there will be nations

which did not receive the mark of the beast, who will
enter into the Messianic Kingdom with Christ. Although
Satan will be chained at that time, the human heart
will remain the same in those who are born during the
Millennium. The Bible is very clear that many children
will be born during the Millennial Age, and these, of
course, will have to be regenerated just exactly like any
others in this present dispensation. However, open sin
will be immediately punished in the Millennial Age,
but there will undoubtedly be a great number who will
give outward obedience to the Lord Jesus Christ, but
will not within their own hearts accept Him. This will
constitute the great army which Satan will marshal at
the end of the Millennial reign in order to oppose the
Lord Jesus Christ. A child will not reach the age of
responsibility until he reaches a hundred years, and so
will not be punished before that age.

**272. Please explain to me the meaning of the 65th and 66th
    chapters of Isaiah.**

This is too large an order to be answered in a letter.
This passage of Scripture is written to Israel. They are
God's charge against the Nation who had forsaken His
law and His commandments, had gone after strange
gods, had indulged in idolatry, and had eaten of unclean
meats such as swine and other creatures which were
definitely prohibited for Israel by the law. The rest
of the chapter, of course, tells how the Lord is going
to forgive them, and settle them in the Land in the end
time. You realize that these restrictions upon Israel
concerning certain meats are not for us in this Age of
Grace today.

273. In one of your messages you state that "Christ laid aside the form of God, was cradled in a virgin's womb and was born in blood and pain." In Isaiah 66:7 it reads, "Before her pain came she was delivered of a man child." From this I thought Christ would be delivered without labor pain. Have I misunderstood it?

Before she travailed, she brought forth; before her pain came, she was delivered of a man child (Isa. 66: 7).

I do not believe that Isaiah 66:7 refers to the virgin Mary in any sense whatsoever. If you will look very carefully at verse 8 of this 66th chapter of Isaiah you will notice that he is talking about Zion and the Nation of Israel. In the succeeding verses, 9-11, you will also see that he is talking about the Nation of Israel who was to bring forth the man child according to Revelation 12:1, 2.

Since the Bible clearly teaches that Jesus became like unto us in ALL things, sin only excepted, we must believe that He also in His birth became like unto us, or else this could not be fulfilled. I am sure that if you will carefully read the context of Isaiah 66, you will see that the reference is to the conversion of Israel, which is still largely in the future.

274. What is the meaning of the "wheels within the wheels" in Ezekiel 1:16-21?

I must confess that this is one of the many, many passages in the Bible I do not understand. Rather than speculate, I admit my ignorance.

275. How do you reconcile the passage in Ezekiel 18:24 with the teaching of "eternal security"?

But when the righteous turneth away from his righteousness, and committeth iniquity, and doeth according to all

> the abominations that the wicked man doeth, shall he live?
> All his righteousness that he hath done shall not be men-
> tioned; in his trespass that he hath trespassed, and in his
> sin that he hath sinned, in them shall he die (Ezek. 18:24).

Do not forget that Ezekiel 18:24 was written under the dispensation of the law, and certainly does not harmonize with the teachings of the grace of God in the New Testament. I will admit that it is not an easy verse to reconcile, and many attempts have been made to explain its meaning away. However, you are thoroughly familiar with the rule that we are never to allow a text whose exposition is uncertain to influence us concerning any others which are absolutely clear and positive. Permit me to say I have never preached on Ezekiel 18:24, and I shall myself need just a bit more light before I attempt it.

276. In Ezekiel 28:12-15, who is the King of Tyrus?

> Son of man, take up a lamentation upon the king of
> Tyrus, and say unto him, Thus saith the Lord GOD; Thou
> sealest up the sum, full of wisdom, and perfect in beauty.
> Thou hast been in Eden the garden of God; . . .
> Thou art the anointed cherub that covereth; and I have
> set thee so: thou wast upon the holy mountain of God;
> thou hast walked up and down in the midst of the stones
> of fire.
> Thou wast perfect in thy ways from the day that thou
> wast created, till iniquity was found in thee (Ezek. 28:12-15).

The King of Tyrus was a type of Satan, and not Satan himself. Many, many times the Lord uses in the Bible certain individuals to represent other personalities. I believe for instance that Nimrod, the hunter of souls in Genesis 10, was a type of the coming Antichrist, as well as many others. The Lord therefore refers first of all to the King of Tyrus and his oppression, and then uses it as a stepping stone for the revelation concerning the sin of Satan.

277. Who are the shepherds mentioned in Ezekiel 34?

The shepherds spoken of in Ezekiel 34 are not the Gentiles, but are the false teachers and priests of Israel who had led the people astray. If you will read the chapter carefully, you will notice that the context indicates that this refers to Israel's leaders. We believe that it has reference also to the false teachers in Israel today, who are causing God's people to reject the Messiah, the Lord Jesus Christ, whereas He came to be their Saviour.

278. Are the battles mentioned in Ezekiel 38 and Revelation 19 one and the same?

The battle of Ezekiel 38 is fought between Russia and her allies and the United Nations, about the MIDDLE of the Tribulation period.

Revelation 19, however, records the Battle of Armageddon in which all nations will be engaged at the END of the Tribulation.

279. I have a question concerning Ezekiel, chapters 40 to 48. Is this the description of the new Jerusalem where the saved shall live and reign a thousand years with Christ? Will we again go back to those burnt offering sacrifices when Christ reigns?

The New Jerusalem as mentioned in Revelation will be the eternal abode of the saints of God, and will not come down from Heaven until after the thousand years are finished. During the thousand years the Lord Jesus Christ will reign over the earth with His Church, and then after the final rebellion of Satan has been put down, the New Jerusalem will descend.

In regard to the sacrifice and burnt offerings during the Millennial Age, this will be for Israel only, during the reign of Christ. It will be a memorial, just as we today have the Lord's Supper in commemoration of our Lord's death. It will not be a sacrifice or ritual of any specific value except as a memorial of the past deliverances of Israel.

280. **In the last few chapters of the Book of Ezekiel we are told of the building of the Temple, and also the dividing of the Land among the twelve tribes; also the mode of worship, and almost a complete resumption of the old temple worship, even to the day of atonement, a sin offering (Ezekiel 45:23) and the feasts.**

    We are told that there is one offering for sin (the Lamb of God). Is God taking Israel back to the place where they left Him, or is it a memorial to Israel as the Lord's Supper is to the Church?

Concerning the last few chapters of Ezekiel, we believe that the Temple at Jerusalem is going to be restored again, and the Old Testament worship and many of the sacrifices will be re-instituted, not as a PROPHECY of the coming Redeemer, but only as a MEMORIAL, pointing back to the Cross of Christ. We have for the Church the Lord's Supper which is the memorial of His death, and we believe that in the same way Israel when the Land is divided again among the tribes, will celebrate the memorial of the Messiah by these methods. They will, of course, be entirely fulfilled as types, but will only look back to the days of their deliverance.

281. In reading Daniel 3:23 I was impressed with the fact that Daniel is not mentioned. Where was Daniel when the three men were cast into the furnace?

> And these three men, Shadrach, Meshach, and Abed-nego, fell down bound into the midst of the burning fiery furnace (Dan. 3:23).

The Bible does not tell us definitely where Daniel was at the time, but it is presumed that he was probably ministering in the court of the king as the cup-bearer. The Holy Spirit has seen fit not to tell us why Daniel did not say something, or intercede for these young men, but when we get to glory I am sure that we shall understand.

282. In Daniel 11:3-20, to whom does this refer?

I believe that this refers to the northern powers headed up by Russia, who will swoop down upon the Land of Israel after the Rapture, in the Tribulation time. Also there is no question that the Man of Sin is definitely referred to in this same 11th chapter. He was, of course, typified by Antiochus Epiphanes.

283. In studying my Bible I have come across two verses which are hard for me to reconcile. How can "many" in Daniel 12:2 be the same as "every man" in Romans 2:6?

> And MANY of them that sleep in the dust of the earth shall awake, some to everlasting life, and some to shame and everlasting contempt (Dan. 12:2).
> Who will render to EVERY MAN according to his deeds (Rom. 2:6).

Concerning Romans 2:6 where God speaks to EVERY MAN and Daniel 12:2 where the word MANY is used, I have never had any difficulty with this, since I believe that the sense of Daniel 12:2 is rather "THE many," than merely MANY. The expression MANY does not exclude ANY, but rather gives the information that the ALL consists of "many" or a "great number."

284. Could Joel 2:12 be used to prove that it is Scriptural to fast?

> Therefore also now, saith the LORD, turn ye even to me with all your heart, and with fasting, and with weeping, and with mourning (Joel 2:12).

This does not apply to us now, but will be after the Church is gone, after the Rapture, and during the Tribulation period; and I do not believe that the fasting there is for us right now.

285. I was told that the verses in Amos 8:5 and 9 had reference to the changing of the Sabbath to the first day. Is this correct?

> Saying, When will the new moon be gone, that we may sell corn? and the sabbath, that we may set forth wheat, making the ephah small, and the shekel great, and falsifying the balances by deceit?
>
> And it shall come to pass in that day, saith the Lord GOD, that I will cause the sun to go down at noon, and I will darken the earth in the clear day (Amos 8:5, 9).

I do not believe that this has any reference whatsoever to the change of the sabbath to the first day. In fact, the sabbath has never been changed; it is still the seventh day of the week and not the first, and is not for Christians but only for Jews. We celebrate the Lord's Day and the resurrection day, and have nothing to do with the sabbath whatsoever.

286. I was wondering as I read Zechariah 5:1-4, if the appearance of "flying saucers" could be the fulfillment of this passage?

Then I turned, and lifted up mine eyes, and looked, and behold a flying roll.

And he said unto me, What seest thou? And I answered, I see a flying roll; the length thereof is twenty cubits, and the breadth thereof ten cubits.

Then said he unto me, This is the curse that goeth forth over the face of the whole earth: for every one that stealeth shall be cut off as on this side according to it; and every one that sweareth shall be cut off as on that side according to it.

I will bring it forth, saith the LORD of hosts, and it shall enter into the house of the thief, and into the house of him that sweareth falsely by my name: and it shall remain in the midst of his house, and shall consume it with the timber thereof and the stones thereof (Zech. 5:1-4).

I do not find anything in Zechariah, chapter 5, to indicate that the reference there is to the so-called "flying saucers" of today. I am afraid we are in danger of reading something into the Scriptures which the Holy Spirit never meant to be there. Of course, as you realize, we don't even know what the "flying saucers" are; but I do not believe that we have a right to make this interpretation from Zechariah until we have more evidence. We must be very careful that we do not jump to conclusions and become a reproach in wild speculation, when we ought to be true to the Word of God. We need not resort to sensationalism in proclaiming the Word of God.

287. What is the book of remembrance mentioned in Malachi 3:16?

Then they that feared the LORD spake often one to another and the LORD hearkened, and heard it, and a book of remembrance was written before him for them that feared the LORD, and that thought upon his name (Mal. 3:16).

I do not believe that we need to take this as a literal "book of remembrance." The same is true of the "book of life." It is undoubtedly a figure of speech, and represents the fact that the Lord knows everything and keeps a record of everything, and everything will be rewarded. Whether it is a literal book or symbolic, of course, makes no difference, because God is omniscient. I therefore believe that either interpretation would be correct. If one wishes to think of it as a literal book, I do not see any objection, while on the other hand, it need not necessarily be so.

CHAPTER XIV

PROBLEMS AND PERPLEXITIES
ON PUZZLING PASSAGES
(Part II—New Testament)

288. Even though Matthew, Mark, and Luke are dated A. D. 33, and John A. D. 30, they record the same incidents. Am I correct in this? Also is there another record of Jesus cleansing the Temple?

There is a difference of opinion as to whether there were one or two cleansings of the Temple. There are those who believe that the record in John 2 was at the beginning of our Lord's ministry, and the three records in Matthew, Mark, and Luke were at the close of His ministry here upon the earth. Then there are others who believe that all four of them refer to the same cleansing. Personally, I lean toward the former interpretation, that there was a cleansing earlier in His ministry, and another later on. However, it is one of those things which after all is not important, and we may have to see our Lord in order to find out the correct interpretation. As you probably know, the dates given by the translators of our Bible are only approximate dates, and they are not to be taken to be exact in all cases.

187

289. Please explain Matthew 5:22. Is this man saved or lost?

> But I say unto you, That whosoever is angry with his brother without a cause shall be in danger of the judgment: and whosoever shall say to his brother, Raca, shall be in danger of the council: but whosoever shall say, Thou fool, shall be in danger of hell fire (Matt. 5:22).

I am afraid that I am not sufficiently informed to give you a positive answer. There are many, many things in the Bible which remain mysteries now, and it is best to wait, and to occupy ourselves with those things which are clearly and definitely revealed. I am sorry that I cannot give you a more definite answer on Matthew 5:22, but I would not want to be dogmatic on something that I am not perfectly clear on myself. (Read Deuteronomy 29:29.)

290. What is the meaning of Matthew 6:3?

> But when thou doest alms, let not thy left hand know what thy right hand doeth (Matt. 6:3).

Our Lord here is talking especially about hypocrisy, and doing religious acts just for the sake of being seen. He was speaking to the Pharisees who liked to stand on the market places and the corners of the streets going through their religious motions and devotions in order that they might be respected by men. The Lord therefore says that when we do these things we should not do them in order to be seen by others, but only because of our relationship to Him. What He means by not letting "thy left hand know what thy right hand doeth" is that we are to serve Him, to worship Him, and even in our giving, do it only as unto Him, and not in order to be appreciated by men.

291. I am unable to reconcile Matthew 7:22 with Mark 9:38-40. Can you give me some help on this?

Many will say to me in that day, Lord, Lord, have we not prophesied in thy name? and in thy name have cast out devils? and in thy name done many wonderful works? (Matt. 7:22).

And John answered him, saying, Master, we saw one casting out devils in thy name, and he followeth not us: and we forbad him, because he followeth not us.

But Jesus said, Forbid him not: for there is no man which shall do a miracle in my name, that can lightly speak evil of me.

For he that is not against us is on our part (Mark 9:38-40).

You must remember that Mark 9:38-40 is speaking of people who were believers in the Lord Jesus Christ, and were preaching Him, but just didn't happen to belong to the same crowd of the apostles, and this was the occasion for the criticism of the disciples, that because he didn't belong to their own group, he should be stopped from preaching and doing these wonders in the name of Christ. However, the Lord rebukes them, because this is sectarianism. We do not all have to belong to the same group, as long as we are faithfully seeking to exalt the Lord and to do His will. Then we are members of One Body, and interested in one program. It is the Lord's own way of condemning the sectarian spirit of being unwilling to cooperate with others just because they do not happen to belong to our own church and our own denomination.

However, in Matthew 7:22 we have quite another situation. These people had never known the Lord Jesus Christ. As you will notice from verse 21, they had made a profession of Him, and had even prophesied in His Name, but they had never experienced a saving relationship with Him. They may have used the name of Jesus doing these miracles, but they were not with Him at all.

Remember the magicians in Pharaoh's day were able to duplicate the miracles performed, but they certainly were not of the Lord. We believe that the Devil is also able to perform miracles and to do signs and this may be the explanation of Matthew 7.

292. In Matthew 8:22, what is the meaning of the phrase, "let the dead bury their dead"?

We must first see the connection in which Jesus told His disciple to "let the dead bury their dead." The entire verse in Matthew 8:22 reads as follows:

> But Jesus said unto him, Follow me; and let the dead bury their dead (Matt. 8:22).

If you want to be My disciple, says Jesus, you must be willing to subject EVERYTHING to Me, placing Me before everything else, no matter how important other things may seem, even the burial of your own father, if that becomes necessary. Now, of course, we do not believe that Jesus meant that we are not to give due respect to our loved ones, and there certainly is no harm in burying one's father; but Jesus tested him to see if he was willing to go all the way with Him. The business of a disciple is not burying dead people, but raising the dead by the Gospel of the grace of God.

293. I am not at all clear on the passage in Matthew 11:12-15. Are Elijah and John the Baptist the same person?

> And from the days of John the Baptist until now the kingdom of heaven suffereth violence, and the violent take it by force.
>
> For all the prophets and the law prophesied until John.

And if ye will receive it, this is Elias, which was for to come.

He that hath ears to hear, let him hear (Matt. 11:12-15).

When Christ came the first time, He offered Himself as the King of Israel, but was rejected. As a result the Kingdom was not established, but postponed until His Second Coming. The Lord knew all of this from eternity, even though He came and offered the Kingdom to Israel. As a result we have two comings of the Lord Jesus Christ; and since the King is to be heralded by a forerunner, and that forerunner will be Elijah when the Lord comes the second time, the Lord sent John the Baptist instead at His first coming. If the Nation of Israel had accepted Christ at His first coming, Elijah would have come in person to herald the coming of the Lord Jesus. However, since God knew that they would not receive His Son, He sent John the Baptist instead, who was the "Elijah" of the first coming, and who according to Scripture came in the spirit of Elias. If you will look carefully at Matthew 11:14, you will notice, "And if you will receive IT, this is Elias, which was for to come." Note the little word IT is in italics, and should be left out; and what the Lord really is saying is this: "If you will receive him, this would have been Elias, which was for to come." However, the Lord knew they would not receive Him, and so John the Baptist came instead of Elijah. When the Lord comes the second time it will be Elijah himself, according to Malachi 4 and Revelation 11.

294. Please explain the meaning of the man with the unclean spirit in Matthew 12:43-45.

When the unclean spirit is gone out of a man, he walketh through dry places, seeking rest, and findeth none.

Then he saith, I will return into my house from whence

I came out; and when he is come, he findeth it empty, swept, and garnished.

Then goeth he, and taketh with himself seven other spirits more wicked than himself, and they enter in and dwell there: and the last state of that man is worse than the first. Even so shall it be also unto this wicked generation (Matt. 12:43-45).

You must remember that this is a parable which was spoken by the Lord Jesus Christ to show that reformation is not enough. A person may clean himself up morally and religiously, but unless he receives the Lord Jesus Christ into his heart, it will do him no good at all. That is the meaning of this man in whom the evil spirits had been abiding. That is the picture of a sinner. Merely putting out the evil spirits without receiving someone to take their place is absolutely worthless, and therefore the "last state of that man is worse than the first."

295. A few days ago I received a letter from a Roman Catholic priest. He said, "Matthew 16:18 was spoken in Aramaic, not Greek. PETROS and PETRA are both the same word 'kepha' in Aramaic." He also said that "Hebrews 10:11, 12 was written of the Mosaic sacrifices, not of the Mass." How would you answer this man?

And I say also unto thee, That thou art Peter, and upon this rock I will build my church; and the gates of hell shall not prevail against it (Matt. 16:18).

And every priest standeth daily ministering and offering oftentimes the same sacrifices, which can never take away sins:

But this man, after he had offered one sacrifice for sins for ever, sat down on the right hand of God (Heb. 10:11, 12).

As we all know, the original manuscripts are not available, and all we have are translations of the original.

We therefore can only speculate as to the details of the original manuscripts. Why the Lord should have left the originals to be lost we do not know, and maybe one of these days He will allow them to be discovered, and then all of these questions will be settled. Since we therefore do not have access to the original, it is entirely a matter of speculation and tradition when this man says that the portion in Matthew was spoken in Aramaic and it did not make the distinction between "petra" and "petros."

I believe that the best answer to the claims of the Roman Catholic Church is found in the International Bible Encyclopedia under the heading of "Matthew's Gospel." All of our Greek translations as well as the Concordance and Bible Encyclopedias make the distinction of Matthew 16:18 very clear. If you have access to the International Bible Encyclopedia, I refer you to Item 3 under the heading "Matthew's Gospel," at the bottom of page 2010.

This same thing applies to Hebrews 10:11, 12 in stating that it was written of the Mosaic sacrifices, and not of the mass. Of course, the writer of Hebrews knew absolutely nothing about a "mass" in those days, and it is entirely an innovation and authenticated only by the voice of the Roman Catholic Church. Whatever they may teach concerning Peter and the mass, it is all negated by the rest of the Scriptures. These men do not refer to Peter's own words, but just harp over and over again on the one passage in Matthew 16. If they would carefully read I Peter 2:4-8 and I Corinthians 3:11 and other passages, they would know just exactly what the true teaching of the Word of God is. Since we are to build our faith NOT ON TRADITION, but on the "what saith the Scriptures," I do not feel that these statements by the Roman Catholic priest carry any weight whatsoever.

296. I am unable to understand the meaning of the words in Matthew 16:28, that "there be some standing here, which shall not taste of death, till they see the Son of man coming in his Kingdom." I do not see how this is possible, since these words were written so long ago.

> Verily I say unto you, There be some standing here, which shall not taste of death, till they see the Son of man coming in his kingdom (Matt. 16:28).

It is impossible to go into a detailed study of this passage without writing a book, so I trust a brief explanation will be helpful. Chapter 16 of Matthew should never have been made to close at this point, for chapter 17 begins with the conjunction "and." This links the first verse of Matthew 17 with the last verse of chapter 16. Matthew 17:1 is an uninterrupted continuation of chapter 16. Verses 1 and 2 of chapter 17 are the answer to the statement of Jesus that "some standing here shall not taste of death, till they see the Son of man coming in his kingdom."

> And after six days Jesus taketh Peter, James, and John his brother, and bringeth them up into an high mountain apart.
>
> And was transfigured before them: and his face did shine as the sun, and his raiment was white as the light (Matt. 17:1, 2).

After six days Jesus took the three disciples and showed them as clear a picture, as concise, as full a picture of the glorious coming Kingdom of Christ as is given anywhere in the Bible. The transfiguration was the fulfillment of Jesus' promise that He would show to some of His disciples the glory of His Kingdom reign.

297. Please explain Matthew 20:1-16. Does this mean our rewards?

There is nothing in the parable of the laborers in the vineyard in Matthew 20 that would lead us to believe that this has anything to do with rewards at all. The parable was spoken in order to emphasize the sovereignty of God in giving to each one according as He purposes and that no one has a right to ask God what He is doing. The matter of rewards is very definitely taught in other passages of Scripture, such as I Corinthians 3 and II Corinthians 5:10. All those that belong to the Lord are saved, but we will be judged as to our works and our opportunities and will receive our rewards on the basis of that. This is also taught in the parable of the pounds and of the talents.

298. In Matthew 24:13, what does Jesus mean by the expression, "he that shall endure to the end shall be saved?"

But he that shall endure unto the end, the same shall be saved (Matt. 24:13).

This passage deals with the Tribulation period, after the Rapture of the Church. The context clearly indicates it has its primary application to Israel during the "time of Jacob's trouble" and speaks of those Jews who will be sealed against destruction when thousands of others will be slain. Those who shall endure will be saved for their reign with the Messiah. This verse cannot be applied to Christians today without completely ignoring the simplest rule of Bible interpretation; namely, "contextual interpretation." This passage refers to the chil-

dren of Israel, and the faithful remnant. As the Bible
teaches that great numbers of unbelieving Israelites will
perish during these Tribulation days, and only the
remnant will be saved, it refers to those who will not
perish in the Tribulation period, but shall come through
it safely. I do not believe that this ever refers to the
matter of salvation, but rather the matter of passing
through the Tribulation period in order to go into the
Kingdom Age with their Messiah and Christ, the Lord
Jesus. In Revelation 7 we find this company of 144,000
sealed in their foreheads, and kept safe so that they shall
not perish.

299. To what event does Matthew 24:27, 28 refer?

> For as the lightning cometh out of the east, and shineth
> even unto the west; so shall also the coming of the Son of
> man be.
> For wheresoever the carcase is, there will the eagles be
> gathered together (Matt. 24:27, 28).

This passage is a reference to the coming of the Lord
and the fact that where the body is, there God's people
will be gathered together. The word "carcase" here can
also be translated "body."

300. How do you explain the passage in Matthew 24:36 in the light of John 10:30?

> But of that day and hour knoweth no man, no, not the
> angels of heaven, but my Father only (Matt. 24:36).
> I and my Father are one (John 10:30).

In regard to Matthew 24:36 and John 10:30, both
are true. As God, Jesus knew everything and was one
with God. As a man, He bore the limitations of humanity.

301. **It seems there is a contradiction between Matthew 24:40 and Luke 17:34. How can Christ come while the people are working, and also at night when they are sleeping?**

> Then shall two be in the field; and one shall be taken, and the other left (Matt. 24:40).

> I tell you, in that night there shall be two men in one bed; the one shall be taken, and the other shall be left (Luke 17:34).

There is absolutely no contradiction here. You must remember that while it is daytime here, it is nighttime in China; and when it is midday in England, it is morning here in the United States. Since the earth is round, and there is a certain part of the earth which is always in the darkness of night while the other part is in the light of day, this presents no problem at all. When Christ comes, there will be those who will be sleeping because it will be night in the part of the earth where they live, while others will be living where it is morning, and others where it is the middle of the day.

302. **Please explain the meaning of the phrase, "cut him in pieces and appoint him his portion with the unbelievers" as found in Matthew 24:51 and Luke 12:46.**

> And shall cut him asunder, and appoint him his portion with the hypocrites: there shall be weeping and gnashing of teeth (Matt. 24:51).

> The Lord of that servant will come in a day when he looketh not for him, and at an hour when he is not aware, and will cut him in sunder, and will appoint him his portion with the believers (Luke 12:46).

I personally do not know exactly what the expression, "cut him in pieces and appoint him his portion with the unbelievers," really means. Scholars take it to mean one of three things: (1) that he never was saved in the

first place; (2) that he was saved and lost his salvation;
or (3) that he was a child of God and will be judged
for his unfaithfulness. I do not accept the first two
views, but believe that he was a child of God, and that
he will have to answer for his unfaithfulness at the
Judgment Seat of Christ. Just exactly what the "cutting
in pieces" means I do not know, but the real point of
the parable is that we must not delay the Lord's coming.
If we believe in eternal security, there can be no other
interpretation but that the Lord has some severe judgment for those who are found unfaithful in spite of the
light which they have received.

303. To which judgment does the verse in Matthew 25:41 have reference?

> Then shall he say also unto them on the left hand,
> Depart from me, ye cursed, into everlasting fire, prepared
> for the devil and his angels (Matt. 25:41).

The judgment in Matthew 25:41 is one of the most
difficult passages in the Scriptures, and many Bible
teachers are not at all agreed as to the proper interpretation. There are those who believe that this is the judgment of the nations, and that they will be judged at that
time as to their treatment of the brethren, referring
undoubtedly to the children of Israel.

However, I believe that this is an individual, personal
judgment of folks who have gone through the Tribulation period, and are now to be judged as to their right
to enter into the Kingdom Age which is to follow. There
are some difficulties with every interpretation, and maybe
we will have to wait until the time when Jesus comes
before we understand it thoroughly. However, I do
not believe that the saved are going to appear at the
Great White Throne, but the wicked only. It is very

definite from Revelation 20 that the first resurrection is completed before the judgment of the Great White Throne takes place.

304. In Matthew 26:29, to what does the word "new" refer?

> But I say unto you, that I will not drink henceforth of this fruit of the vine, until that day when I drink it NEW with you in my Father's kingdom (Matt. 26:29).

Concerning the drinking of the fruit of the vine in his Father's kingdom, you must remember that this refers to the fact that the Lord Jesus would not sit down with His disciples again until after His Second Coming, and therefore it would be NEW in the sense that it would not be a memorial of His death, but a fulfillment of His promise of His coming again.

305. Is there a contradiction between Matthew 27:5 and Acts 1:18? Please explain.

> And he cast down the pieces of silver in the temple, and departed, and went and HANGED HIMSELF (Matt. 27:5).
>
> Now this man purchased a field with the reward of iniquity; and FALLING HEADLONG, he burst asunder in the midst, and all his bowels gushed out (Acts 1:18).

There is no contradiction between these two passages. Matthew tells us Judas "strangled" himself, and the writer of Acts adds that after that, he fell down the cliff. The Book of Acts merely adds a detail not given in Matthew.

306. Is the Lord's commission given in Matthew 28:18-20 for the Church today?

> And Jesus came and spake unto them, saying, All power is given unto me in heaven and in earth.
>
> Go ye therefore, and teach all nations, baptizing them

in the name of the Father, and of the Son, and of the Holy Ghost:

Teaching them to observe all things whatsoever I have commanded you: and, lo, I am with you alway, even unto the end of the world. Amen (Matt. 28:18-20).

This was our Lord's parting commission to the eleven disciples, in which He gave them their particular commission to go forth and to preach the Gospel of the Lord Jesus Christ, and to baptize those who believed and received their testimony. This, of course, was given to the apostles, and went first of all to the Nation of Israel; but we believe that this commission also extends to us today, so that it is our business in fulfillment of His will, to go into all the world as we are trying to do by radio now, and preach the Gospel to all men. This is the desire of our Lord, and we believe that the fact that we have the radio today is an indication of the nearness of His return, and the fulfillment of this job.

307. In Mark 6:8, 9 why were the disciples told not to take a change of clothing?

And commanded them that they should take nothing for their journey, save a staff only; no scrip, no bread, no money in their purse:

But be shod with sandals; and not put on two coats (Mark 6:8, 9).

The context of this passage clearly indicates that the disciples had a job to do which must be done in a great hurry, and they should not be impeded by any extra baggage. It is a picture of the urgency of sending out the Gospel of the Lord Jesus Christ, and to allow nothing to hinder us because the time is so short in which we have to labor.

308. Please explain Mark 11:23, 24, especially in the light of the teaching of "divine healing."

For verily I say unto you, That whosoever shall say unto this mountain, Be thou removed, and be thou cast into the sea; and shall not doubt in his heart, but shall believe that those things which he saith shall come to pass; he shall have whatsover he saith.

Therefore I say unto you, What things soever ye desire, when ye pray, believe that ye receive them, and ye shall have them (Mark 11:23, 24).

In this passage I believe that the Lord was speaking here both literally and figuratively. Undoubtedly if we had faith like a grain of mustard seed, we should be able to do much greater things, but the Lord is evidently not speaking only of removing literal mountains, but mountains of a spiritual nature. If the "divine healers" quote this text to support their claim that everything is possible by faith, then we would appreciate it greatly if they would remove a few mountains and prove their point. It is easy to quote a text out of its connection, but it is more difficult to back it up with actual experience.

309. Does the 13th chapter of Mark refer to the time after the Rapture of the Church? If so, where do we find the Scripture for this? Also please tell me what is meant by the 17th verse of this chapter.

But woe to them that are with child, and to them that give suck in those days! (Mark 13:17).

I believe that the entire 13th chapter of Mark refers to the Tribulation which will come upon this earth AFTER the Rapture of the Church, and will continue until the Second Coming of Christ. This entire picture seems to be centered in the Land of Palestine, and has to do with the Jewish nation rather than with the Gentiles or the Church.

In the 17th verse the reference is again to the Land of Palestine in the Great Tribulation, and to the Jewish mothers. It will be such a time of sorrow that those who are at that time expecting, and have to flee will be subjected to greater suffering than at any other time. This is made clear by verse 19 when it says that there shall be such affliction, such as was not from the beginning of the creation, neither shall be again. I therefore sincerely believe that this has nothing to do with the Church whatsoever, but applies entirely to the Jewish nation, and especially in the Land of Palestine.

310. What is the meaning of the parable of the patched garment and the old bottles as recorded in Luke 5:36-39?

> And he spake also a parable unto them; No man putteth a piece of a new garment upon an old; if otherwise, then both the new maketh a rent, and the piece that was taken out of the new agreeth not with the old.
>
> And no man putteth new wine into old bottles; else the new wine will burst the bottles, and be spilled, and the bottles shall perish.
>
> But new wine must be put into new bottles; and both are preserved.
>
> No man also having drunk old wine straightway desireth new: for he saith, The old is better (Luke 5:36-39).

Concerning the parables of the patched garment and the old bottles (or "skins" as it is in the original), I believe that the reference here is to LAW and GRACE. The old garment is the dispensation of the LAW and the new patch is the GRACE of God. The same thing is true of the old bottles (the Law) and the new wine (the grace of God). They simply cannot mix, and do not go together, but have to be kept separate in the plan of salvation. I think that this is the primary interpretation, although as you suggest, it may have an application in referring to the new birth by the Spirit of God.

311. In the passage in Luke 7:36-50 do you think that the sinful woman referred to is Mary Magdalene?

I am afraid that I cannot solve the problem of the woman in Luke 7:36-50. There are some that believe she may have been Mary Magdalene, but there is no absolute and definite evidence whatsoever.

312. Do you think that the seven devils that Christ cast from Mary Magdalene, mentioned in Luke 8:2, were seven sins?

> And certain women, which had been healed of evil spirits and infirmities, Mary called Magdalene, out of whom went seven devils (Luke 8:2).

We believe that the devils which were cast out of Mary Magdalene were actual, literal "demons," and did not represent sins.

313. In Luke 11:4, please explain the meaning of the phrase, "lead us not into temptation."

> And forgive us our sins; for we also forgive every one that is indebted to us. AND LEAD US NOT INTO TEMPTATION; but deliver us from evil (Luke 11:4).

There are a number of interpretations of this petition. The one which I favor is to read instead of "lead us not into temptation," KEEP US FROM TEMPTATIONS. There are other expositors who believe that it means "keep us safe in temptations." I am aware that it is beset with some difficulties, but we certainly do not believe that the Lord deliberately leads His people to be tried and tempted, as we know from the experience of Job and Abraham and others as well. The following phrase, "but deliver us from evil," should correctly read "deliver us from THE EVIL ONE." The entire prayer, therefore, seems to indicate that it is a petition to restrain the Devil from placing temptations upon us beyond our ability to bear. In this connection I believe that we also ought to read I Corinthians 10:13,

> There hath no temptation taken you but such as is common to man; but God is faithful, who will not suffer you to be tempted above that ye are able; but will with the temptation also make a way to escape, that ye may be able to bear it (I Cor. 10:13).

314. Does the word "immediately" in Luke 12:36 mean that all believers will not be raptured?

> And ye yourselves like unto men that wait for their lord, when he will return from the wedding; that when he cometh and knocketh, they may open unto him immediately (Luke 12:36).

You suggest that at Jesus' coming NOT ALL believers will open to Him immediately because they are not ready. I do not believe that it refers to a part of the Bride going through the Tribulation period. This, I think, is stretching things too far. The word IMMEDIATELY here means "a prompt response to His call," and corresponds to the suddenness of His appearing and our rapture, as also expressed in I Corinthians 15.

315. Who is the unfaithful servant in Luke 12:46?

> The lord of that servant will come in a day when he looketh not for him, and at an hour when he is not aware, and will cut him in sunder, and will appoint him his portion with the unbelievers (Luke 12:46).

We must place the emphasis here upon the word PORTION. The judgment which the Lord will bring upon the unfaithful servants will, of course, stem from the same holiness and justice of God which will also condemn the sinner in the end time. However, the rest of the passage is so clear that this is a servant of the Lord, that it is unthinkable that he could possibly be lost. The reason this parable is quoted in both Matthew and in Luke is undoubtedly for the purpose of emphasis, in order to stress the importance of this particular truth concerning the delaying of the Lord's return.

316. In Luke 15, does the parable of the Prodigal Son refer to a sinner or a backslidden Christian?

I have always felt that the parable of the Prodigal Son is a parable first of all of salvation, and not one that is to be applied to the backslider. In fact, the three parts of the one parable in Luke 15 all have to deal with Christ's answer to the accusation of the Pharisees in the beginning of the chapter, when they found fault with Him because He ate with publicans and with sinners.

It was in order to illustrate that He came "to seek and to save that which was lost" (Luke 19:10) that He gives the three parts of the one parable: the Lost Sheep, the Lost Coin, and the Lost Son. Of course, I believe that while the primary interpretation is to sinners, that we have a right also to make the application to backsliders.

317. Please explain Luke 16:1-10.

In this parable of the unjust steward, I must honestly confess that this is one of the passages of Scripture that I am not clear on myself, especially the 9th verse, which is one which presents a great deal of difficulty, and therefore I would rather not give my opinion, for fear I might give the wrong interpretation.

The general teaching of the parable, however, is a

warning to faithfulness, that whereas the unjust steward had to pay for his deeds, so too we are responsible to the Lord for that which has been committed to our trust. Beyond this application, I am not prepared to go. There are many things in the Bible which we do not yet understand, but we do learn day by day, and some day we "shall know as we are known."

318. Please explain to me the meaning of the verse in Luke 16:9.

Make to yourselves friends of the mammon of unrighteousness; that when ye fail, they may receive you into everlasting habitations (Luke 16:9).

To understand this verse, we must take the entire passage in its context. I am very frank to admit that it is full of difficulties which are not clear. However, you will notice from the context in this chapter that the Lord is speaking about an unjust steward, and the wise move which he made in providing for the future. When he found that he was going to lose his position, he did something which, while we may not recommend it from the standpoint of honesty, was nevertheless a shrewd move because he made friends of his debtors, so that when he was put out of his position, he would have someone to turn to. I believe that the moral of this story of the unjust steward is that he was at least wise even in his injustice, to make preparation for the inevitable future.

It is in this connection that this ninth verse occurs, and the Lord tells us to make friends of the "mammon of unrighteousness." The word MAMMON means "riches" and the word UNRIGHTEOUSNESS undoubtedly refers to the things of this world. The expression appears to mean simply this, "use your money with an eye to the future," as the steward did his. Use your money in such a way that your expenditures shall not stand in account against you, and be a witness against you in the life to come. I believe the teaching is that we are responsible for that which the Lord entrusts to our care, and so we are to use it even in a wicked world in such a way that it may bring forth the commendation of our Lord when He comes.

I realize that this does not fully explain the expression, "that when ye fail, they may receive you into everlasting habitations." As long as we are not too sure of our ground in the matter of the exposition of this verse, I believe that it is well to caution against some errors that might be encountered. Let us first of all beware of supposing by the use of money we can purchase to ourselves God's favor, and forgiveness of sins. Heaven, of course, is not to be bought. I do not believe that we can read any such interpretation into this verse. But on the other hand, we must also recognize the fact that our conduct here will have a bearing on our rewards at the Judgment Seat of Christ. I therefore believe that this verse teaches among other things that a right use of the material things of this world for right motives will be for our benefit in the world to come. It will not justify us, but it will be an evidence of our faithfulness, which shall receive the commendation of our Lord.

319. What is the meaning of Luke 18:8?

> I tell you that he will avenge them speedily. Nevertheless when the Son of man cometh, shall he find faith on the earth? (Luke 18:8).

I am sure that the Lord is speaking here about the conditions on the earth when He comes again at the end of this age. It speaks of the apostasy and the awful falling away and wickedness which will be present upon the earth when the Lord comes. We believe that right today this is already coming to pass in the awful coldness of the Church, and the awful iniquity which is present in the world. Some translations render the closing phrase, "Will he find THE faith on the earth."

320. In Luke 21:36, who are those who will be "counted worthy to escape"?

> Watch ye therefore, and pray always, that ye may be accounted worthy to escape all these things that shall come to pass, and to stand before the Son of man (Luke 21:36).

From the context in Luke 21 it is clear that this must refer to the Tribulation, and that the Church will be taken out before that time. The Lord speaks here about a certain group of people who will be spared from going through the Great Tribulation and time of trouble. Since there are only three kinds of people in the world (Jews, Gentiles, and the Church of God) we know that it must refer to the Church. The Jews will go through the Tribulation, while the Gentiles will be judged in the Tribulation, and only the Church will not pass through, and thus will "escape all these things that shall come to pass."

321. In Luke 22 the Lord says that the twelve apostles would sit upon twelve thrones to judge the twelve tribes of Israel. Was Judas included in this number?

I personally do not feel that Judas was included in this twelve, but rather that the Apostle Paul has taken the place of Judas Iscariot. Judas was in the twelve in order to fulfill the purpose of God, but I do not believe that in the plan and the purpose and program of God he ever was an apostle in the sense of being a saved man.

I do not therefore believe that Judas will be among the twelve who will judge, because "he went unto his own place" according to Acts 1:25, and will never show up in the Kingdom nor in Heaven.

322. To what future time does Luke 23:29-31 refer?

For, behold, the days are coming, in the which they shall say, Blessed are the barren, and the wombs that never bare, and the paps which never gave suck.

Then shall they begin to say to the mountains, Fall on us; and to the hills, Cover us.

For if they do these things in a green tree, what shall be done in the dry? (Luke 23:29-31).

This is a picture of the Tribulation period. After the Church has been called out, there will come upon the earth a time of great trouble, sorrow, and these words apply to that period. I do not believe that they have any application to the days in which we are living right now. In this same connection it might interest you to read carefully Matthew 24, verses 16 and 18, where we also have a description of that awful time of the Tribulation, and these passages can only be interpreted in the light of that revelation.

323. Is there any spiritual significance in the fact that there is no mention of parables in John's gospel?

This is incorrect, for Jesus did speak one parable in John (read John 10:1-6). Concerning the significance that there is mention of only one parable recorded by John, it is entirely in harmony with the purpose of the Gospel through John. Matthew was written particularly to the Nation of Israel, and therefore contains a large number of signs and parables. Mark was written particularly for the Romans of that day, and therefore contains more of the acts and the deeds of the Lord Jesus

Christ. Luke is the physician who wrote especially for the Greeks, and therefore gives us the scientific aspect of the Gospel, while John wrote to show forth the Lord Jesus Christ as the eternal, pre-existent Son of God, as contained in the very first verse of John:

> In the beginning was the Word, and the Word was with God, and the Word was God (John 1:1).

For this reason Jesus did not cause the parables to be recorded in John as they are in the other gospels.

324. What is the difference between the "only begotten" in John 1:14 and "the firstbegotten" Son of God in Hebrews 1:6?

> And the Word was made flesh, and dwelt among us, (and we beheld his glory, the glory as of the ONLY BEGOTTEN of the Father,) full of grace and truth (John 1:14).
>
> And again, when he bringeth in the FIRSTBEGOTTEN into the world, he saith, "And let all the angels of God worship him" (Heb. 1:6).

The expression, "the only begotten of the Father," speaks of the eternal, pre-existence and co-existence of the Lord Jesus Christ with the Father. It is, of course, a mystery which we cannot understand, and we shall probably have to wait until we get to Heaven, before we can get the full revelation concerning this particular statement.

The same thing is true of the term "firstbegotten." It is usually understood that this refers to His resurrection, and in relation to the Church. It has nothing to do with the fact that Christ is the eternal, pre-existent Son of God. Again it is one of those things upon which we cannot be too dogmatic.

325. In John 2:4, what did Jesus mean by this?

> Jesus saith unto her, Woman, what have I to do with thee? mine hour is not yet come (John 2:4).

This must be taken in the light of the fact that Jesus had renounced every human tie in His obedience to do the Father's will. This was not in any way disrespect for His mother, but only the declaration that He had come to do the will of His Father, and He would not allow anything, not even the most precious and dearest ties, to stand in the way of the accomplishment of that purpose.

326. How do you harmonize Hebrews 11:5 with John 3:13? I have always believed that Enoch, Moses, and Elijah were translated to Heaven without seeing death, and that they came to visit Jesus on the Mount of Transfiguration.

> And no man hath ascended up to heaven, but he that came down from heaven, even the Son of man which is in heaven (John 3:13).
>
> By faith Enoch was translated that he should not see death; and was not found, because God had translated him: for before his translation he had this testimony, that he pleased God (Heb. 11:5).

You are quite mistaken in regard to having believed that Enoch, Moses, and Elijah were translated into Heaven without having seen death. The Bible very definitely states that Moses died upon Mount Nebo, and that the Lord buried him, and no man knew his grave. At some subsequent time he must have been raised from the dead, because he appeared together with Elijah on the Mount of Transfiguration.

You are also mistaken in your statement that Enoch was among those who came to visit Christ on the Mount

of Transfiguration. I am afraid that you have not carefully read your Bible, and therefore I want to correct
you in this: only Enoch and Elijah were translated, and
Enoch did not appear on the Mount of Transfiguration.

There is no conflict between Hebrews 11 which records
the translation of Enoch, and John 3:13. The Lord
here is speaking of His ascension into Heaven to sprinkle
the blood upon the mercy seat, and it has nothing at all
to do with the translation of the others. Just exactly
where Enoch and Elijah went is not fully revealed.

327. In John 13:1, what is the meaning of the word "hour"?

> Now before the feast of the passover, when Jesus knew
> that his hour was come that he should depart out of this
> world unto the Father, having loved his own which were
> in the world, he loved them unto the end (John 13:1).

I have always been of the opinion that the "hour"
which Jesus spoke of was the hour of victory, when He
should ascend into Heaven, and sprinkle the blood of
atonement upon the mercy seat, and complete the work
of redemption. This is very evident from the words
that he "should depart out of this world unto the Father."
I do not see how any other interpretation can be placed
upon it.

328. Concerning John 16:23, is this verse for us today?

> And in that day ye shall ask me nothing. Verily, Verily,
> I say unto you, Whatsoever ye shall ask the Father in my
> name, he will give it you (John 16:23).

John 16:23 is for us today, but it is not without qualifi-
cations. We must never take a verse by itself, but we must
remember that other verses in the Bible also have a
bearing on every other part of Scripture. It is true that
we can ask whatsoever we will in the name of the Lord

Jesus and receive it, IF we pray according to God's will, and if it is His will to give it to us. We simply cannot ask for anything that we want, but it must be according to the will of God, and if in His counsel it is good for us. We must always remember that all of the Scripture must be taken in its entirety, and we must not build upon one verse alone. I realize that this verse is used by some unscriptural healers to claim that anything can be received of the Lord, but we must remember that it must be in accord with His will. Even the Lord Jesus prayed, "Not my will, but Thine, be done" (Luke 22:42).

329. Why did Jesus forbid Mary Magdalene to touch Him, and then later the same day invite Thomas and the disciples to touch Him?

> Jesus saith unto her, Touch me not; for I am not yet ascended to my Father: but go to my brethren, and say unto them, I ascend unto my Father, and your Father; and to my God, and your God (John 20:17).

Concerning Mary Magdalene who was told not to touch the Lord Jesus Christ, you will notice that in the rest of the verse it says, "for I am not yet ascended to my Father: but go to my brethren, and say unto them, I ascend unto my Father." From this passage it appears that Jesus on the first resurrection day must have ascended unto the Father, for Mary Magdalene was not allowed to touch Him because of that very reason. However, that same night He invited the disciples to handle Him and see, so that He must have finished the work, and sprinkled the blood on the mercy seat during that day.

330. In Acts 2:39, please explain especially "for the promise is unto you, and to your CHILDREN."

> For the promise is unto you, and to your children, and

to all that are afar off, even as many as the Lord our God
shall call (Acts 2:39).

You must remember that in Acts 2 there are no Gentiles present, only Jews and proselytes. The promise
in Acts 2:39 is to national Israel—not the Church, and
refers to the Abrahamic covenant of Genesis 15 and 17.

331. Is the commission in Acts 8:15-17 still binding today?

Who, when they were come down, prayed for them, that
they might receive the Holy Ghost:
(For as yet he was fallen upon none of them: only they
were baptized in the name of the Lord Jesus.)
Then laid they their hands on them, and they received
the Holy Ghost (Acts 8:15-17).

You must remember that this is the last stage in the
commission which the Lord gave to His disciples when
He commanded them that they were to begin at Jerusalem, and Judea, and in Samaria, and unto the uttermost
parts of the earth. The Gospel first went to the Jews at
Pentecost in Jerusalem; and then the next stage, it
had to go to Samaria. For this purpose Peter, who had
the use of the keys of the Kingdom, was sent to Samaria,
and also laid his hands upon them. Later on in the
tenth chapter of Acts, we have the third stage in this
commission, "unto the uttermost parts of the earth."
In this case it was a Gentile, Cornelius, and they also
received the signs of the giving of the Holy Spirit.

However, we believe that after the Gospel had gone
to the Jews in Samaria, it now is to be proclaimed
throughout all the earth, and these apostolic signs ceased
and we are only expected to believe. The laying on of
hands, we believe, also to have been an apostolic ministry,
and to have ceased after the revelation of the Bible was
complete.

332. Does Acts 8:20 teach that a believer can be lost?

> But Peter said unto him, Thy money perish with thee, because thou hast thought that the gift of God may be purchased with money (Acts 8:20).

There is nothing in this passage whatsoever that would establish the doctrine of losing one's salvation. When Peter said to Simon, "Thy money perish with thee," he explains it later on, when he tells him that he had made the great mistake of supposing that the gift of God could be purchased with money. However, we also know that Simon repented of his sin, and we believe that he was forgiven. We must never base our interpretations on a questionable passage of Scripture, but must confine our doctrinal conclusions to those which are absolutely definite.

333. According to Acts 15:16-18, will the literal Tabernacle be rebuilt?

> After this I will return, and will build again the tabernacle of David, which is fallen down; and I will build again the ruins thereof, and I will set it up:
> That the residue of men might seek after the Lord, and all the Gentiles, upon whom my name is called, saith the Lord, who doeth all these things.
> Known unto God are all his works from the beginning of the world (Acts 15:16-18).

I do not believe that we need to take the word "tabernacle" in this passage literally. I believe that the tabernacle of David is a term, a symbol, used to signify the setting up of the Kingdom during the Millennial reign of the Lord Jesus Christ. Whether the literal Tabernacle will be rebuilt we do not know, but we do know that it is a definite prediction concerning the return of Christ, and the setting up of His Kingdom here upon the earth. Beyond this, I do not believe that we ought to go.

334. In Acts 16:3, why did Paul circumcise Timothy?

> Him would Paul have to go forth with him; and took and circumcised him because of the Jews which were in those quarters: for they knew all that his father was a Greek (Acts 16:3).

The answer is given right in the verse, "because of the Jews." This is the reason. Paul, of course, did not consider that circumcision was necessary, but in order not to offend the Jews, he had Timothy circumcised. This was in line with Paul's policy, that he had become all things unto all men. To the Jews he had become a Jew; to those who were under the law, as under the law; to those that were free from the law, as being free from the law (I Corinthians 9:19-22). Paul did not do it because he felt it essential, but rather in order to prevent any disturbance of misunderstanding. There is a serious question in my mind about the wisdom of Paul's action. It dangerously suggests a compromise.

335. What is the meaning of the last part of the verse in Acts 17:26?

> And hath made of one blood all nations of men for to dwell on all the face of the earth, and hath determined the times before appointed, and the bounds of their habitation (Acts 17:26).

I am of the opinion that Paul is referring to the fact that there are no different races in the world, but only one human race. There are different nationalities and peoples and tribes and tongues but we are all of Adam's blood, and therefore the blood in all nationalities is the same, and there is no basic difference. The various groups and nationalities were distributed by God in their particular geographic locations.

336. In Acts 17:26 Paul speaks of "all nations being of one blood" but the marginal note says the word "blood" is omitted from the best manuscripts. Adam and Eve being our first parents, when and how has the change taken place in the blood of the colored and white? Was Ham, the son of Noah, the first Negro?

I would point out first of all that there is no good reason why the word "blood" in Acts 17:26 should be left out. The simple fact that the word is omitted in some of the manuscripts does not mean that it should not be there. Scientific developments today have proven that the blood in all of humanity is exactly the same. We know, for instance, today that we can transfuse blood from a Negro to a white man or from a Chinese into an Englishman, and it does not affect either their personality or their appearance, physically or mentally in any way whatsoever. It is today an established fact that there is no difference in the blood of the different nationalities.

We believe, therefore, that the Negro has developed this pigment in his skin because of being exposed to the sun for many, many generations, and thus he has finally acquired his dark color. It is possible for white men to be exposed to the sun so much that they become as brown as a nut, and some of them almost as dark as a Negro. If this were to be repeated generation upon generation the skin undoubtedly would become permanently pigmented.

Ham was definitely not the first Negro, but was just the same color as his brothers, Shem and Japheth; but because of their geographic distribution these various physical and mental characteristics have developed over a period of many centuries. You realize, of course, that there is only one RACE, which is the fallen human race of Adam, and the Bible never distinguishes between races, but rather between nationalities, tongues, people, and tribes.

337. Does Romans 13:2 mean that we can lose our salvation?

> Whosoever therefore resisteth the power, resisteth the ordinance of God: and they that resist shall receive to themselves damnation (Rom. 13:2).

In this passage you must remember that Paul is talking about the obedience of Christians to the laws of the state under which they live. What Paul is saying here is simply this, that if we do not obey the laws of the land, then we can expect to receive judgment. The word "damnation" here has nothing to do with salvation, but means rather the "punishment" which the laws of the land will inflict upon us.

338. I would like to have a better understanding of the meaning of the word "carnality" as used in the Scripture. Its meaning in Romans 15:27 seems to conflict with its use in other passages.

> It hath pleased them verily; and their debtors they are. For if the Gentiles have been made partakers of their spiritual things, their duty is also to minister unto them in carnal things (Rom. 15:27).

The word "carnality" must always be taken in the context in which it is used. As Paul uses it in the first part of I Corinthians, it evidently refers to spiritual pride, which is the product of the natural mind and of the flesh. The passage in Romans 15:27 does seem to conflict with the general interpretation; but if you remember that spiritual pride is the result of the flesh and the Adamic nature, it can also be made to apply to the material things of this life. I believe that the context ought to determine which interpretation we are to place upon the particular passage. Romans 15:27 refers to material things, without any moral connotation.

339. In the Book of I Corinthians, why is the portion pertaining to woman's hair applicable now, and not the gifts to the church?

Bobbing or cutting of a woman's hair has nothing at all to do with the special gifts and manifestations to the Church at Corinth. By reading carefully chapters 12, 13, and 14 of I Corinthians, you will notice that Paul is not particularly interested in endorsing these gifts, but rather in the correction of their abuse and placing them in their proper place.

340. What is the significance of I Corinthians 1:10-16?

Now I beseech you, brethren, by the name of our Lord Jesus Christ, that ye all speak the same thing, and that there be no divisions among you; but that ye be perfectly joined together in the same mind and in the same judgment.

For it hath been declared unto me of you, my brethren, by them which are of the house of Chloe, that there are contentions among you.

Now this I say, that every one of you saith, I am of Paul; and I of Apollos; and I of Cephas; and I of Christ.

Is Christ divided? was Paul crucified for you? or were ye baptized in the name of Paul?

I thank God that I baptized none of you, but Crispus and Gaius;

Lest any should say that I had baptized in mine own name.

And I baptized also the household of Stephanas: besides, I know not whether I baptized any other.

Paul the Apostle, in this passage is condemning the spirit of sectarianism, a spirit of following man rather than the Scriptures. There was a great division in the church at Corinth, because some followed after Paul, others Apollos, and others Peter, and some who were holier than all the rest prided themselves in saying they were "of Christ" only. This spirit of sectarianism and denominationalism is a great sin. There were some in Corinth who were priding themselves on the fact that Paul had baptized them, and this made them feel superior to everyone else. Paul condemns this very, very severely; and while he does not deny that he baptized some of them, he is trying to emphasize the fact that while baptism is an act of obedience on the part of the believer, it certainly is not the most important thing in salvation.

341. What is meant by "defiling the Temple of God" in I Corinthians 3:17?

> If any man defile the temple of God, him shall God destroy; for the temple of God is holy, which temple ye are (I Cor. 3:17).

Since our bodies are God's temples, this passage means that the Lord will destroy those PHYSICALLY who continue to live in open and unconfessed sin. This again has nothing to do with salvation, but rather the judgment of God, according to I Corinthians 11, in visiting those who are disobedient with sickness and with weakness, and sometimes even with death. Again let me repeat, it has nothing to do with salvation.

342. Please explain the fifth chapter of I Corinthians.

This was a man who was living in deliberate open sin, and because he would not repent, he had to be excommunicated from the assembly, and turned over to the judgment of God.

343. What is the meaning of the expression, "a dispensation of the Gospel," as found in I Corinthians 9:17?

> For if I do this thing willingly, I have a reward: but if against my will, a dispensation of the gospel is committed unto me (I Cor. 9:17).

You must remember the context in which this was given. Paul is speaking here about the fact that those who preach the Gospel have a right to live of the Gospel; that is, those who are engaged in full time Gospel service ought to be supported in that ministry. You will notice this in verse 14,

> Even so hath the Lord ordained that they which preach the gospel should live of the gospel (I Cor. 9:14).

However, Paul in order that no reproach might be brought upon his ministry had refused to take anything whatsoever for his services, but rather was willing to labor with his hands in order to make his own living that none might say that he was doing this for his own personal benefit. He rendered his service as a thank-offering unto the Lord, and expected absolutely nothing in return. Then he goes on to say that he is under restraint, and that he must preach the Gospel, and that he cannot do anything else. Then comes verse 17, where he tells us that if he does this willingly and gladly, the Lord will give him a reward, but if he does it only because he has to, and not because he wants to, he still is given the Gospel to be preached, but will not receive a reward. This undoubtedly is what he means by a "dispensation" or a special provision committed unto him in this preaching. It is then that he says in the

18th verse that when he preaches the Gospel without charge, he will not abuse the power of the Gospel.

344. What is the meaning of I Corinthians 11:16?

> But if any man seem to be contentious, we have no such custom, neither the churches of God (I Cor. 11:16).

This merely means that if people disagree with Paul in regard to his teaching concerning a woman and long hair, it makes no difference because after all the churches do not have any such custom, and they ought to abide by the teaching of the Word of God.

345. Please explain I Corinthians 14:35.

> And if they will learn anything, let them ask their husbands at home: for it is a shame for women to speak in the church (I Cor. 14:35).

This is Paul's admonition to the Christian women in the assembly of Corinth, that they were not to take any leading part in the public meetings, and of course they were not to preach or teach in the place of men. This does not mean that they have no place in the assembly for praying and for working and for testifying. They were not to take any place of authority or prominence, but to ask their husbands at home concerning things which they could learn there, rather than burden the church with it.

When Paul says that it is a shame for a woman to speak in the church, he is not talking about testifying or praying, but he is referring especially to preaching and taking the place of authority.

346. I am puzzled over the meaning of the words "die daily," found in I Corinthians 15:31. I would appreciate any help you can give me on this.

> I protest by your rejoicing which I have in Christ Jesus our Lord, I die daily (I Cor. 15:31).

Concerning Paul "dying daily," you must remember that Paul in the context is speaking of the sufferings that he had endured for the sake of the testimony of Christ, and the dangers to which he was constantly exposed as he moved among his enemies. He was therefore in jeopardy of his life every day, and he could say that he did "die daily." I do not believe that the context here means that he died to self daily, although this is also true, but rather that he was in danger of death everywhere he went, because of his faithfulness to the Lord.

347. How do you explain the "last trump" of I Corinthians 15:52, if the Church is raptured before the Tribulation? Are there not seven trumpets to follow during this period? How can the Rapture be the last trump?

> In a moment, in the twinkling of an eye, AT THE LAST TRUMP: for the trumpet shall sound, and the dead shall be raised incorruptible, and we shall be changed (I Cor. 15:52).

Paul here is talking about the Church, and not the Tribulation. This trump is the last trump for the Church, but not for the world. If I have a dinner bell which I ring when dinner is ready, it calls my children to come. It is the last call for dinner. But it has nothing to do with my neighbor's children. They must wait for their own dinner bell. So too, the last trump for the Church in I Corinthians 15 has nothing in common with the seven trumpets of judgment in Revelation. The first trump brings a message of joy; the second is a message of judgment.

348. There is a United Oneness Pentecostal Church near where we live who practice I Corinthians 16:20. Should this be followed today?

> All the brethren greet you. Greet ye one another with an holy kiss (I Cor. 16:20).

I do not believe that this is a command to be followed as a rule. Undoubtedly, in those days when there was so little fellowship and so much persecution, the custom was to greet one another with a holy kiss, but I do not see any evidence of its continuation, since it does not constitute a command for the Church. However, if they feel that this is the will of the Lord, I certainly would raise no objection to it. "Let every man be fully persuaded in his own mind."

349. Two passages of Scripture have been of concern to me. They are Galatians 5:4 and Hebrews 12:15. From these two verses it would seem we could lose our salvation.

> Christ is become of no effect unto you, whosoever of you are justified by the law; ye are fallen from grace (Gal. 5:4).
> Looking diligently lest any man fail of the grace of God (Heb. 12:15a).

The passage in Galatians 5:4 must be read entirely in the context of the entire epistle. In Galatians Paul is attacking the false doctrine that a person is saved by grace and then kept by his own works; so in the entire epistle he proves that we are not only saved by the power of God, but we are also KEPT by the power of God. Of course, the very fact that we are saved by grace makes its demands upon us, and therefore we are to live our lives accordingly. That is why chapter 5 of Galatians begins with the words, "Stand fast therefore in the liberty wherewith Christ hath made us free." If we go back again under the bondage of the law, it does not mean that we can fall from salvation, but we have fallen from the truth of grace, and there will undoubtedly be a loss of rewards at the Judgment Seat of Christ. It is not a matter of losing our salvation, but the expression here, "fallen from grace," means that we have turned our back upon those truths which can make us most fruitful for Him. The same thing is implied in Hebrews 12:15. Notice it says FAIL *of* the grace of God.

Of course, if these were the only two verses dealing with this subject in the Bible we might easily suppose that they taught falling away from salvation, but we must look at all these things in the light of the entire Scriptures, and the rest of the Bible very definitely teaches that when we are saved by the grace of God, we can also expect to be kept by the power of God.

350. If we are in the Body of Christ, and not in the Kingdom, what did Paul mean in Colossians 1:11-14?

Strengthened with all might, according to his glorious power, unto all patience and longsuffering with joyfulness;

Giving thanks unto the Father, which hath made us meet to be partakers of the inheritance of the saints in light:

Who hath delivered us from the power of darkness, and hath TRANSLATED US INTO THE KINGDOM of his dear Son:

In whom we have redemption through his blood, even the forgiveness of sins (Col. 1:11-14).

Concerning this passage and the matter of the Kingdom, you must remember that the Kingdom is spoken of in various aspects in the Bible.

First of all, we speak of the Kingdom of God, which includes the entire rule and dominion of God over His entire creation. Then we speak of the Kingdom of Heaven which is, strictly speaking, the reign of the King, the Lord Jesus Christ, upon the earth during the Millennial period. Then too the Bible speaks about the mystery of the Kingdom, which is this present age, during which the Church is being called out. In this sense we who are in the Body of Christ are also in the Kingdom, and undoubtedly this is what Paul is referring to here. As the King is part of the Kingdom, so too the Bride is also a member of the Kingdom.

351. **In speaking on verses 11 and 12 of Colossians 2, our pastor said that these verses show that baptism has taken the place of circumcision, which also includes our children. I cannot agree with him, but cannot explain why. Please help me.**

> In whom also ye are circumcised with the circumcision made without hands, in putting off the body of the sins of the flesh by the circumcision of Christ:
> Buried with him in baptism, wherein also ye are risen with him through the faith of the operation of God, who hath raised him from the dead (Col. 2:11, 12).

In these verses in which both circumcision and baptism are mentioned, there is nothing which gives anyone any reason to believe that circumcision was replaced by baptism. Just because the two words occur in the same verse certainly does not give anyone the right to say that one has replaced the other. Moreover, baptism is not sprinkling, but immersion, and if baptism of infants has taken the place of circumcision, then there is no reason why girl babies should be baptized.

The whole infant sprinkling error is a hangover from

the Catholic Church without one single verse in the Bible to support it. It might be well to ask your pastor to give you one single verse in the entire Bible where is says definitely that babies should be baptized. He will probably have to resort to the catechism to prove his point, but he certainly will not be able to do it from the Scriptures.

352. Please explain Colossians 2:20.

> Wherefore if ye be dead with Christ from the rudiments of the world, why, as though living in the world, are ye subject to ordinances (Col. 2:20).

I believe that this entire passage must be read in the light of Galatians 2:19, 20 which says:

> For I through the law am dead to the law, that I might live unto God.
>
> I am crucified with Christ: nevertheless I live; yet not I, but Christ liveth in me: and the life which I now live in the flesh I live by the faith of the Son of God, who loved me, and gave himself for me (Gal. 2:19, 20).

Paul is speaking here about those who have been delivered and freed from the law, and are now standing and walking in the liberty of grace. He therefore admonishes them not to become entangled again with the yoke of works and bondage, and a negative religion as expressed in "Touch not; taste not; handle not" (Col. 2:21), but to serve the Lord out of a heart of gratitude and thanksgiving unto Him. You will notice that in verse 22 of Colossians 2 he says that these all are to perish with the using; and they are the commandments and doctrines of men.

He is warning these Colossian believers not to place themselves again under the bondage of legalism, but to walk in the freedom of the Spirit, and give their worship

not by coercion or by commandment, but out of a
heart of gratitude and love and devotion for His great
salvation.

353. From the verses in I Thessalonians 4:16 and 5:2, would it be right to assume that Christ is coming in the night?

For the Lord himself shall descend from heaven with a
shout, with the voice of the archangel, and with the trump
of God: and the dead in Christ shall rise first (I Thess.
4:16).

For yourselves know perfectly that the day of the Lord so
cometh as a thief in the NIGHT (I Thess. 5:2).

The figure of Jesus coming as "a thief in the night"
does not say that He IS coming in the night, but He is
coming AS a thief in the night. This means that He
will come secretly while the world is not aware of it, and
will snatch away His Bride in the twinkling of an eye.

354. Could the passage in I Timothy 5:23, 24 be used as God's approval for drinking wine?

Drink no longer water, but use a little wine for thy
stomach's sake and thine often infirmities.

Some men's sins are open beforehand, going before to
judgment; and some men they follow after (I Tim. 5:23, 24).

It is very evident that Timothy must have been suffering from some kind of a stomach ailment, and Paul here
is advising Timothy to take a little wine medicinally
once in a while for his condition. The word for "wine"
in this particular verse happens to be the same word
elsewhere used for fermented wine, and therefore was
to be taken as a medicine. This, of course, does not
give anyone a right to use it for beverage purposes. If
your name is Timothy, and you have stomach trouble
and many infirmities, it might help you to take a

LITTLE WINE under doctor's orders; but remember, it says a LITTLE WINE, NOT as a BEVERAGE, but as a MEDICINE.

355. I would like to know what the words in II Timothy 2:12 mean?

> If we suffer, we shall also reign with him: if we deny him, he also will deny us (II Tim. 2:12).

I believe that this means just exactly what it says, that if we are going to try and live all out for the Lord Jesus Christ, we will be misunderstood, and probably have to suffer difficulty from those who do not believe in our precious Saviour; but we will also receive a special place of reward in the reign of Christ.

356. I believe that we are now seeing some of what is mentioned in II Timothy 4:3, 4 today, but I would like to have your views on this.

> For the time will come when they will not endure sound doctrine; but after their own lusts shall they heap to themselves teachers, having itching ears;
> And they shall turn away their ears from the truth, and shall be turned unto fables (II Tim. 4:3, 4).

I too believe that we are living in the very days of which Paul is speaking. There is today a great deal of frothiness in Gospel preaching, and much superficiality. People do not seem to be interested in the solid meat of the Word of God any more, but are looking for all sorts of entertainments and musicals and Hollywood antics, instead of the sound doctrine of the Word of God. We believe that this is a definite sign of the end of the age, and only makes us more eager for the coming of the Lord.

The "itching ears" I believe refers to the people who

listen and are desiring teachers who shall entertain them rather than feed them on the strong meat of the Word of God.

357. What is the meaning of Hebrews 1:6? Does this mean that before Jesus came down to be born in our world, the angels all bowed down to worship Him?

> And again, when he bringeth in the first begotten into the world, he saith, And let all the angels of God worship him (Heb. 1:6).

This is usually interpreted as referring to the coming into the world of the Lord Jesus Christ. He is, of course, the firstbegotten of the Father, and when He came into the world, it was God himself in the person of the Lord Jesus Christ who came in human form. As you know from the record in Luke and in Matthew, He was accompanied by angels who heralded His arrival, and told the shepherds about the coming of the King.

358. What is the meaning of "perfection" as found in Hebrews 6:1? Are we to try to be perfect?

> Therefore leaving the principles of the doctrine of Christ, let us go on unto perfection; not laying again the foundation of repentance from dead works, and of faith toward God (Heb. 6:1).

In this verse the word "perfect" means "to be mature" or "grown up." What the apostle is saying is that we ought not to remain by the mere essentials and basic truths of the Word, which are for young Christians; but we should continue to study and grow in grace until we reach the maturity of manhood. The Hebrew Christians were underdeveloped babes in Christ, and are admonished to grow up, according to Hebrews 5:12-14,

> For when for the time ye ought to be teachers, ye have need that one teach you again which be the first principles

of the oracles of God; and are become such as have need of milk, and not of strong meat.

For every one that useth milk is unskilful in the word of righteousness: for he is a babe.

But strong meat belongeth to them that are of full age, even those who by reason of use, have their senses exercised to discern both good and evil (Heb. 5:12-14).

359. Please explain Hebrews 6:1-6.

Therefore leaving the principles of the doctrine of Christ, let us go on unto perfection; not laying again the foundation of repentance from dead works, and of faith toward God,

Of the doctrine of baptisms, and of laying on of hands, and of resurrection of the dead, and of eternal judgment.

And this will we do, if God permit.

For it is impossible for those who were once enlightened, and have tasted of the heavenly gift, and were made partakers of the Holy Ghost,

And have tasted the good word of God, and the powers of the world to come,

If they shall fall away, to renew them again unto repentance; seeing they crucify to themselves the Son of God afresh, and put him to an open shame (Heb. 6:1-6).

This is one of the deeper passages of the Word of God, and cannot be dealt with in just a few sentences, or even pages. You must remember that the sixth chapter of Hebrews must be interpreted in the light of the last two verses of the fifth chapter in which we read:

For every one that useth milk is unskilful in the word of unrighteousness: for he is a babe.

But strong meat belongeth to them that are of full age, even those who by reason of use have their senses exercised to discern both good and evil (Heb. 5:13, 14).

The sixth chapter, therefore, begins with an admonition that we are to go on, and grow up unto perfection. The word "perfection" means "maturity" or to be grown up in the faith, and means that we should not continue to be babes who can only take the milk of the Word, and are not able to take the heavier doctrines. Then he gives some of these simple doctrines of baptism, laying on of hands, etc., and then goes into the passage that is most difficult to explain. Personally, I believe that the passage of Hebrews 6:4-6 has to do with Christians who have turned their backs upon the light that God has given them, and therefore have to suffer at the Judgment Seat of Christ. I do not believe that it deals with salvation, but rather with the matter of rewards when Jesus comes.

I would advise that you keep on studying and reading, and pray that the Lord may give you light to understand some of the deeper things in the Word of God.

360. What are the "two immutable things" in Hebrews 6:18?

> That by two immutable things, in which it was impossible for God to lie, we might have a strong consolation, who have fled for refuge to lay hold upon the hope set before us (Heb. 6:18).

This refers to "the smoking furnace and burning lamp" in Genesis 15:17. They represent God's justice and His love, which were reconciled on the basis of the sacrifice in Genesis 15, looking forward to the Cross of Christ. Abram had a vision of Calvary in answer to his question, "Whereby may I KNOW that I shall inherit it (the land)?" It is well that we remember the background and the occasion of the answer of God to Abram's request for more assurance. You will recall that God had told him to prepare the slain animals; and while he was fast asleep, God passed between them in the form of a "smoking furnace" and a "burning lamp," thus completing a beautiful picture of reconciliation at Calvary.

God must satisfy His immutable justice in the death of the sinner before His love can be satisfied in the salvation of the sinner. These are the two immutable things mentioned in Genesis 15, the smoking furnace and the burning lamp—the unchangeable JUSTICE and the unchangeable LOVE of God. God's love, unless it is presented against the background of God's righteousness and holiness, becomes a weak and powerless message. His love, the burning lamp, is not sufficient. We must also have the smoking furnace, by which it was impossible for God to save the sinner in any way without satisfying His righteousness as well.

361. Concerning Hebrews 8:10, is this still in the future or has it been fulfilled?

> For this is the covenant that I will make with the house of Israel after those days, saith the Lord; I will put my laws into their mind, and write them in their hearts: and I will be to them a God, and they shall be to me a people (Heb. 8:10).

I am quite sure that this still lies in the future, and has to do with the conversion of Israel. This verse is a quotation from Jeremiah, chapter 31, and the context clearly indicates that it has reference to Israel in the latter days.

362. I am puzzled concerning Hebrews 10:19. Do you think that passage means that we Christians can bring our problems right before God's throne of grace and have God speak to us through the Holy Spirit within our own souls? that we can ask God questions about our daily lives and He will give us the answer of what to do by a sort of "mental telepathy"? I need a clearer understanding of what this verse really means.

> Having therefore, brethren, boldness to enter into the holiest by the blood of Jesus (Heb. 10:19).

Concerning our "coming boldly to the throne of grace," we must remember that the ministry of the Holy Spirit is inseparably linked up with the revelation of the Holy Spirit in the Bible. The Spirit does not speak to us in audible tones, nor through visions or other physical sensations, but He speaks to us through the Word of God. As we therefore study the Word and seek to know God's will, the Spirit witnesses with our spirit, and from the Word gives us the assurance that we have the petitions for which we ask. We can go to the Lord Jesus Christ with every one of our daily problems, no matter how great or small they are, and upon the authority of the Word of God claim an answer to the petition of our prayers, but it must always be according to the Word and according to the will of God.

The witness of the Holy Spirit, therefore, is also the witness of the Word of God. The Holy Spirit witnesses to us by bringing to our attention certain promises from the Book, and assurances on which we base our faith and our hope, and then we have the answer to our prayers. While in days gone by, God spoke through the prophets and through His servants in audible voices and in visions and in dreams and other means of revelation, we do not believe that this is the general order today. God has various ways of communicating with us, and we cannot limit Him, of course, but we do believe that God's general way of speaking to our hearts is through the Word. Therefore, it becomes tremendously necessary that we know the Word and study the Bible, so that we are fully acquainted with God's will.

363. Please explain Hebrews 10:26. Does this refer to saved or unsaved?

For if we sin wilfully after that we have received the

knowledge of the truth, there remaineth no more sacrifice for sins (Heb. 10:26).

I believe this refers to Christians who have had the opportunity of going a long way in the truth of the Gospel of the grace of God, and then have willfully closed their eyes to the light, and have continued in practices and sins which they knew were contrary to the Word of God. I believe that there is a chastening of the Lord for all such, not only in sickness and weakness and even death (I Corinthians 11:28-30), but they will also have to lose their rewards at the Judgment Seat of Christ. I do not believe that this has reference either to the losing of one's salvation, or that it refers to the unsaved. I am sure that it has to do with the chastening of the Lord upon those who willfully and deliberately continue in known and willful sin.

364. In James 5:14 we have mention of "anointing with oil." Does this mean that when we pray for the sick, we should anoint them with oil?

> Is any sick among you? let him call for the elders of the church; and let them pray over him, anointing him with oil in the name of the Lord (James 5:14).

I have always held that this anointing with oil and the prayer of the elders of the church was for a particular and circumscribed class of sickness which was due to unconfessed sin, and therefore represented the chastening of the Lord. I believe that it should be studied in the light of I Corinthians 11, where Paul tells us that because of failure to examine themselves, there were many of the Corinthians weak and sick, and some had even fallen asleep. I believe, therefore, that this particular reference in James has to do with sickness and weakness which has been caused by unconfessed sin. You will notice that it says that the "prayer of faith shall SAVE the sick, and if he have committed sins, they shall be forgiven him" (James 5:15).

Then notice the next word in verse 16 is CONFESS. The entire context, therefore, seems to indicate that it depends upon confession of sin.

As to the anointing with oil, I believe that that is a matter of personal persuasion. If one in praying for the sick wishes to use oil, I personally have no objection, although I do not believe that it is an instruction for universal application. In closing, may I also mention that in this case it has nothing to do with methods of modern divine healers. Here it is not a person going to a "divine healing meeting" and receiving instruction, etc., but here it is the elders themselves going to the sick person, and praying over him.

365. Does the Devil have any part in causing the suffering of believers as mentioned especially in I Peter 1:6, 7; I Peter 4:12; and I Peter 5:10?

> Wherein ye greatly rejoice, though now for a season, if need be, ye are in heaviness through manifold temptations:
> That the trial of your faith, being much more precious than of gold that perisheth, though it be tried with fire, might be found unto praise and honour and glory at the appearing of Jesus Christ (I Pet. 1:6, 7).
> Beloved, think it not strange concerning the fiery trial which is to try you, as though some strange thing happened unto you (I Pet. 4:12).
> But the God of all grace, who hath called us unto his eternal glory by Christ Jesus, after that ye have suffered a while, make you perfect, stablish, strengthen, settle you (I Pet. 5:10).

Concerning the suffering of believers as stated in these passages, I do not think that we have any reason to believe that the Devil has anything to do with the chastening of God's people. We do know that God does permit the Devil sometimes to test God's people, as in the case of Job, but we believe that in this day and dispensation, the Lord permits tribulations and trials in order to strengthen our faith and to prepare us to reign with Him.

I am familiar with the fact that there are certain extreme divine healers who attribute all sickness to the work of the Devil, but I believe this to be absolutely unscriptural, and dishonoring to the Lord, and has no basis whatsoever in the Bible.

366. I am unable to understand the verse in I Peter 4:6.

> For for this cause was the gospel preached also to them that are dead, that they might be judged according to men in the flesh, but live according to God in the spirit (I Pet. 4:6).

If you will look up the original translation for this verse you will find that it should read as follows: "For for this cause was the gospel preached also to them that NOW are dead." The implication is that it was preached to them while they were alive, although now they are dead. I do not know of a better interpretation than this one, although some have tried to read other matters into it.

367. What is the meaning of the Spirit, the water, and the blood, as mentioned in I John 5:8?

> And there are three that bear witness in earth, the Spirit, and the water, and the blood: and these three agree in one (I John 5:8).

It is the general opinion that the Spirit and the water and the blood refer to the Holy Spirit, the Word of God, and the blood of the Lord Jesus Christ. The "water" here is one of the symbols of the Word which is used constantly in Scripture.

368. What is the "sin unto death" mentioned in I John 5:16?

> If any man see his brother sin a sin which is not unto death, he shall ask, and he shall give him life for them that sin not unto death. THERE IS A SIN UNTO DEATH: I do not say that he shall pray for it (I John 5:16).

The "sin unto death" is first of all a sin which only a believer can commit, for John says, "if a BROTHER commits this sin," he does not say that he shall pray for it. It is the sin of continually living in and practicing a known sin against better light and warning. If such sin is not repented of and forsaken, God will sooner or later step in with chastening according to I Corinthians 11:30, which says:

> For this cause many are weak and sickly among you, and many sleep.

Persistent neglect of this chastening may result in death:

> And ye are puffed up, and have not rather mourned, that he that hath done this deed might be taken away from among you (I Cor. 5:2).

The *sin unto death* is the same as the *great transgression* (Psalm 19:13), and *willful sin* (Hebrews 10:26). This sin will be judged at the Judgment Seat of Christ.

369. In the light of the teaching of "divine healing" please explain III John 2.

> Beloved, I wish above all things that thou mayest prosper and be in health, even as thy soul prospereth (III John 2).

There is not the slightest connection here with divine healing. If you will look at the margin of your Bible, you will notice that it should read, "Beloved, I wish

THAT IN all things thou mayest prosper and be in health, even as thy soul prospereth." The fact that John wished that his beloved Gaius might enjoy health was certainly not an excuse for the methods of divine healers today. It only goes to show how hard-pressed they are for proof, when they will pull a passage out of its connection and give entirely the wrong interpretation. This is true of all the Scriptures which they try to use to support their claims.

370. In Revelation 2:9 and also in Revelation 3:9 we read the words, "them which say they are Jews, and are not, but are the synagogue of Satan." Whom do they mean?

> I know thy works, and tribulation, and poverty, (but thou art rich) and I know the blasphemy of them which say they are Jews, and are not, but are the synagogue of Satan (Rev. 2:9).
>
> Behold, I will make them of the synagogue of Satan, which say they are Jews, and are not, but do lie; behold, I will make them to come and worship before thy feet, and to know that I have loved thee (Rev. 3:9).

Concerning those who say they are Jews and are not Jews, I do not wish to be dogmatic, as there are many different interpretations; but I do believe that it applies especially to those who would steal the blessings of the Jews and apply them to themselves, and thus rob the Jew of the promises of the Abrahamic convenant. I am thinking especially of such movements as the Jehovah's Witnesses, who claim they are the 144,000 Jews of the twelve tribes of Israel. As you probably know, the Seventh-day Adventists also claim that they are the 144,-000 Jews and that God is all through with the Nation of Israel as such. Then there are also many churches who spiritualize the prophecies of the Old Testament, and make themselves spiritual Israel, so that God has no more dealings with the Nation of Israel as such.

371. According to Revelation 3:14, was Christ created?

> ...These things saith the Amen, the faithful and true witness, the beginning of the creation of God (Rev. 3:14).

Concerning Jesus being the beginning of the creation of God, this verse must be taken with the rest of the Bible which definitely teaches that Christ is not created, but that He always was. For instance, John 1:1-3 definitely states that Jesus is the Creator, and therefore He existed from eternity before the creation. The passage in Revelation 3:14, therefore, does not mean that Jesus was the first creature, but rather that He is the One who began the creation; that is, that He Himself is the Creator.

372. Could the "come" in Revelation 6:1 be an invitation of salvation?

I believe that the expression "Come and see," which many take as being only COME, is the command to the rider of the white horse to proceed with his program. It could also be translated "Now enter on your mission." Believing as I do that the white horse rider of Revelation 6 is the Antichrist, he of course is restrained by the Holy Spirit and cannot begin his program until he is permitted to. I believe that the primary meaning, therefore, of the "come and see," is that it is spoken to the riders on the horses, giving them the signal when they are permitted to begin their program.

There are also those who believe that the expression "Come and see" was spoken to John. This does carry some weight, because immediately after the first invitation, we read in verse 2, "And I saw." We have the same expression again in verse 5, "And I beheld." This would give some reason to believe that it may have been for John personally. However, I still hold to the fact that it is the word of permission for the riders of the horses to come forth.

373. Who are the "free" men referred to in Revelation 6:15?

> And the kings of the earth, and the great men, and the rich men, and the chief captains, and the mighty men, and every bondman, and every FREE man, hid themselves in the dens and in the rocks of the mountains (Rev. 6:15).

You must remember that these "free" men are referred to in contrast to the ones who are called "bondmen." We believe that at the time of the Tribulation there will be the two ideologies in the world which are existing already today; one represented by Russia, and the other by the free nations. This is a reference to the fact that during that time there will be these two kinds of government on the earth: one which keeps its citizens in bondage, and the other which we know today as free people. I do not believe that it has anything to do with salvation, but entirely those people who are not under the iron heel of despots.

374. Do the 144,000 mentioned in Revelation 7 and again in Revelation 14 refer to the same group?

I have always felt that they are the same identical group. I know that there are some difficulties which are not so easy to explain, but I am convinced after studying it for a number of years that the 144,000 are the firstfruits of the saved Israel during the Tribulation, after the Rapture of the Church. There will be, according to Revelation 7, exactly 12,000 members of each of

the twelve tribes of Israel, who will become the missionaries during that particular age. There will be a special
group of saved Jews who will through their preaching be
the means of the conversion of the multitude of Gentiles
from every people, tongue, tribe, and nation, as described
also in Revelation 7. I do not see any reason at all why
the ones in Revelation chapters 7 and 14 should not be
the same group. In the 7th chapter we are told of the
MINISTRY of the 144,000, while in the 14th chapter we
are told of the CHARACTER of this same group, as
being a specially called and separated company who will
be used of the Lord for the carrying out of His program
during the Tribulation period.

**375. Who are the 144,000 of Revelation 7? I have some
Seventh-day Adventist friends who say they are the
144,000.**

The best way to silence those who claim they belong to
the 144,000 is to ask them to which of the twelve tribes
they belong. The Bible definitely states there were
12,000 of each tribe, and the twelve tribes are all mentioned. The 144,000 are all Israelites, direct descendants
of Jacob, the father of the nation. This claim of the
Adventists is only one of scores of their foolish and absurd
interpretations of the Bible.

**376. Please give me your understanding as to whom the
woman and the child represent as mentioned in the
12th chapter of Revelation.**

There are those who teach that the woman is the
Church. However, I disagree, and believe with all my
heart that the woman here is the Nation of Israel; and
the child who was to rule the nations with a rod of iron
can be none other than the Lord Jesus Christ, according

to Psalm two. It is, of course, a backward look to the birth and ascension of the Lord Jesus that is given to John in the middle of the terrible Tribulation. It is a reminder of the fact that the Lord is the absolute Master of the situation, and the Victor of this combat.

The woman who flees into the wilderness and is protected by the Lord is the Nation of Israel, who under the care of God will be spared from being terminated by the Devil.

377. Who is the "woman" in Revelation 12:6?

> And the woman fled into the wilderness, where she hath a place prepared of God, that they should feed her there a thousand two hundred and three score days (Rev. 12:6).

The woman in this verse I believe to be Israel, and the wilderness is a special place prepared by the Lord, probably in the Land of Moab, where the faithful remnant will be safely sheltered during the Tribulation period.

378. Who are the two beasts mentioned in the 13th chapter of Revelation?

The first beast in Revelation 13 is said to "rise up out of the sea." The sea in Bible symbolism refers to the Gentile nations. This person, therefore, will be a Gentile political ruler, the head of the United Nations of the end time.

The second beast comes out of the earth. It may also be translated "land" and undoubtedly has reference to the Land of Canaan. He will be the religious leader of the end time, the personal Antichrist.

379. Where do we find the word "armageddon" in the Bible?

The word "Armageddon" is found in Revelation 16:16,

> And he gathered them together into a place called in the Hebrew tongue Armageddon (Rev. 16:16).

This is the only place in the Bible where the word is used; although, of course, the "day of the Lord" and the judgments that will come upon the world in the end time are described in many, many other parts of the Bible.

380. Is "the marriage of the lamb" mentioned in the Book of Revelation the same event as the "Rapture of the Church"?

The "Marriage of the Lamb" mentioned in Revelation is NOT the Rapture. The Rapture takes place BEFORE the Tribulation (I Thessalonians 4). The Marriage is AFTER the Tribulation, just before the Second Coming of Christ (see Revelation 19:7-11).

381. Has it ever been established who the beast and the false prophet mentioned in Revelation 19:20 are?

> And the beast was taken, and with him the false prophet that wrought miracles before him, with which he deceived them that had received the mark of the beast, and them that worshipped his image. These both were cast alive into a lake of fire burning with brimstone (Rev. 19:20).

The beast and false prophet are the religious head and the political head of the United Nations after the Rapture of the Church, during the Tribulation period. Their identity will not be revealed until after the Lord takes the Church out.

382. Who are the saints mentioned in Revelation 20:9? Are they earthly people or glorified saints?

> And they went up on the breadth of the earth, and compassed the camp of the saints about, and the beloved city: and fire came down from God out of heaven, and devoured them (Rev. 20:9).

The "saints" which are mentioned in this verse are undoubtedly the members of the elect Nation of Israel who are still in their earthly bodies, and the city is the literal Jerusalem. The glorified Church may also be in view here, for, as we know, they will be reigning with Christ over the earth at that time.

383. What is the meaning of the "commandments" in Revelation 22:14? An Adventist friend of mine has approached me on this passage.

> Blessed are they that do his commandments, that they may have right to the tree of life, and may enter in through the gates into the city (Rev. 22:14).

Your Adventist friend makes the same mistake that all other Adventists do, in believing that every time the word "commandment" occurs in the Bible it must of necessity refer to the Ten Commandments. This is a great delusion, and a terrible mistake. In most cases in the Bible where the words "law" and "commandments" occur, there is no reference whatsoever to the Ten Commandments. When this is the meaning, it is plainly stated that it refers to the commandments written on tables of stone. If you want to know the commandments to which Revelation 22:14 refer, you have but to read I John 3:23 where the Lord Jesus Christ through the Spirit says to the Apostle John, (and through him to us) that:

> ... this is his commandment, That we should believe on the name of his Son Jesus Christ, and love one another, as he gave us commandment (I John 3:23).

This, of course, does not refer to the Ten Commandments, although if we are truly saved we will seek to do God's will, and keep all His commandments. However, these people worship a *day*, and they worship the Ten Commandments, rather than the Lord.

I realize that they are very hard to deal with, since they know practically nothing about the Bible except a few texts which deal with commandments and law and the sabbath day. That is the extent of their knowledge of the Scriptures. The best thing that we can do for them is to continue to be patient and kind, and pray for them that the Lord may open their blind eyes and take away the veil which legalism always places over their eyes.

384. Please explain Revelation 22:15 to me.

> For without are dogs, and sorcerers, and whoremongers, and murderers, and idolaters, and whosoever loveth and maketh a lie (Rev. 22:15).

Concerning the sinners who are outside the gates, this can only refer to the lost who do not have any part in the glorious eternal kingdom of the Lord Jesus Christ, but are shut out, undoubtedly in the place of outer darkness. There are still many things which we have to wait for before we receive the full light, but we thank God that some day we shall "know as we are known."

385. What is the meaning of the word "quickly" in Revelation 22:20?

> He which testifieth these things saith, Surely I come quickly. Amen. Even so, come, Lord Jesus (Rev. 22:20).

There are two ways of explaining this passage. The most common one is that the word "quickly" in the Greek means "suddenly" and the word *quickly* refers to the suddenness with which He will come—IN THE TWINKLING OF AN EYE—rather than to the length of time which will elapse between His promise and His coming.

However, I do not believe that we even need to take this interpretation, since you must remember that it is the Lord speaking. The Bible tells us that WITH THE LORD "a thousand years are as one day." In God's reckoning less than two days (a thousand years each) have passed since He made the promise, and that certainly is not a long while.

In Hosea, chapter 6, the prophet is speaking about the restoration of Israel and says:

> After two days will he revive us: in the third day he will raise us up, and we shall live in his sight (Hosea 6:2).

Since this refers to the Nation of Israel, a day here means a thousand years when Israel will be dispersed, and then in the third thousand years they will be restored in the Land. Personally, I accept the latter interpretation, that we have to take a day as a thousand years in God's reckoning, and the promise, "Behold, I come QUICKLY," presents no difficulty.

Chapter XV

PROPHECY

386. What is the seal of God and the mark of the beast mentioned in the Book of Revelation?

The seal of the living God is some special protection by the Holy Spirit in the Tribulation whereby the people of God will be preserved from the deception of the Anti-christ.

The mark of the beast is a special mark placed on the followers of Satan in the Tribulation. The seal of the living God is NOT sabbath-keeping as Adventists teach, and the mark of the beast is NOT Sunday worship.

387. Will there be sin and sickness during the Millennium, since the Bible tells us that people will die during that time?

You must realize that the Millenial reign with Christ of one thousand years is not to be confused with eternity. In eternity there will be no sin, no sickness, no death of any kind. However, in the Millennium while Christ reigns here upon the earth, there will be no sickness of any kind, but there will be death.

This death will only be in punishment against those who rebel openly against the Lord Jesus Christ, and will be in perfect harmony with His reign of righteousness.

We believe that during the Millennium there will be no poverty, no sickness, no disease; nothing but blessing for those who obey Him. However, if you will read carefully Isaiah 65, from verse 20 to the end of the chapter, I think you will see something of the condition which will prevail during the Millennial period.

In regard to the leaves of the tree of life being for the healing of the nations, this is not to heal them after they are sick, but rather God's means of keeping them from being sick.

388. What is the meaning of the expression—"time, times, and a half a time"?

"Time, times, and a half a time" is equivalent to the 1260 days of Revelation chapter 11, and the 42 months spoken of there. This is the last half of the Tribulation period. The first half of the Tribulation period lasting three and one-half years will be a time of deception, and the last three and one-half years are spoken of as the "Great Tribulation." It corresponds to the last half of Daniel's seventieth week.

389. When will the war with Russia take place?

I am of the firm belief according to Joel, chapters 2 and 3, as well as Ezekiel, chapters 38 and 39, that the final battle with Russia will not take place until after the Rapture. It will probably take place somewhere in the middle of the Tribulation period. Personally, I do not believe that Russia is going to attack the United States, but that her main target is the Land of Palestine. Of course, when that happens, I do believe that the United States will be involved with the other nations against Russia.

390. Will France be included in the Western Confederacy in the restored Roman Empire?

Whatever the developments may be today, this would not alter the teaching of the Word of God. While it is possible that France might for the present temporarily swing toward communism, we believe that in the end when the final conflict comes between the King of the North and the revived Roman Empire, that France will be found among those represented by the ten toes of the feet of the image of Nebuchadnezzar. No matter what conditions prevail as far as current events are concerned, we must believe that the Word of God is still true, and that somehow it is going to come to pass the way it is taught in the Scriptures.

391. What will the saints do during eternity, after the Millennium is over?

This is mostly speculation, and my opinion is no better than others. However, I believe that we, after the Millennium, will spend most of our time on the new earth which the Lord is going to create. I do not believe that God created man in the beginning to be a Heaven dweller, but rather an earth dweller. While we, therefore, will have access to Heaven, I do believe that much of our time will be spent on the new earth, for we will still be human beings, and not angels.

392. Will the young children be caught up in the Rapture?

I am sure that at the Rapture of the Church every single child under the age of responsibility will be caught up to meet the Lord in the air, along with all the adult living believers, as well as the dead in Christ. I do not believe that one of these little children will be left behind. I base this on the fact that Christ died for Adam's sin, and since a little child has no willful sin of its own, it is included in the redemption of Adam, until it definitely rejects the Gospel of the Lord Jesus Christ, and makes its own choice.

We are judged as to what we do with the Lord Jesus Christ, and since a little child is unable to make a decision, I believe that when they die before the age of decision they go directly to Heaven; and so also when Jesus comes, they will go into His presence together with all the rest of the raptured saints. I think that Matthew 18:14 is quite conclusive in this matter:

> Even so it is not the will of your Father which is in heaven, that one of these little ones should perish (Matt. 18:14).

393. Is the United Nations mentioned anywhere in the Bible?

We believe the first attempt at forming a United Nations dates back to Genesis 11. Here Nimrod built a city and a tower for the express purpose of preventing the dispersion of the people upon the earth. It was an attempt to keep all peoples united under one government and one religion. It was an attempt to homogenize the whole human race, but it resulted in confusion and failure.

394. Will Elijah return to the earth before the Rapture? I thought I read something like that in the Bible.

Elijah will return to this earth AFTER the Rapture, but BEFORE the Second Coming. As you know, the Rapture occurs first, followed by seven years of Tribulation, and then the Second Coming of Christ to this earth. It will be during the middle of this Tribulation period that Elijah will return together with Moses. This is prophesied in the last chapter of Malachi, and also given very clearly in Revelation, chapter 11. I believe that the two witnesses in Revelation 11 are the prophets Elijah and Moses.

395. Is there any prophecy which must yet be fulfilled before Christ can return, or is His return the next fulfillment in the order of events?

It is my firm conviction that there is nothing at all in Old Testament prophecy which must still be fulfilled before the coming of the Lord Jesus Christ for His Church. Therefore, I am confident that the Lord might come at any time. Of course, there are a great many Old Testament prophecies as well as New Testament prophecies which have not yet been fulfilled, but these will be fulfilled after the Rapture of the Church and before the Second Coming of the Lord Jesus Christ to this earth. I think that we must understand the difference between the RAPTURE and the SECOND COMING.

First the Lord Jesus Christ comes to take the Church out (THE RAPTURE), and then follows the Tribulation, after which Christ returns WITH His Church (the Second Coming) to set up the Kingdom. The unfulfilled prophecies will therefore occur after the Church has been taken out, during the Tribulation.

396. Will the Jews set up the Sanhedrin again before the Lord returns?

I do not know that there is any Scriptural proof at all for the setting up of the Sanhedrin before Christ comes. Certainly I cannot endorse the theory that this will have to happen before the return of the Lord. That would be saying that the Lord could not return until this happens, and that comes under the heading of delaying the Coming of the Lord which is a very dangerous thing.

397. Do you think that the United States comes under the "Red" rule of the last world government, or does that apply to the so-called "prophetic nations"?

I do not believe that the United States of America will come under the "red" rule of communism. I believe that Russia's aim is entirely in the Middle East, and most particularly Palestine, and that all of these other moves are intended to detract our attention from her real purpose, the Land of Palestine, and the Nation of Israel. I do not believe that the invasion of Palestine will occur until after the Rapture of the Church.

398. What will happen to the earth after the one thousand years of Christ's reign?

At the close of the one thousand years, and after the Judgment of the Great White Throne, this earth will be purified by fire. (Read Revelation 21:1 and II Peter 3:10.)

> And I saw a new heaven and a new earth: for the first heaven and the first earth were passed away; and there was no more sea (Rev. 21:1).
> But the day of the Lord will come as a thief in the night; in the which the heavens shall pass away with a great noise, and the elements shall melt with fervent heat, the earth also and the works that are therein shall be burned up (II Pet. 3:10).

It will not be destroyed in the sense of being annihilated, but will be purified so that all of sin and its results will be burned up, and then we will have the New Heaven and the New Earth.

I also believe that the Land of Palestine will be the eternal and everlasting possession of the redeemed Nation of Israel. We, the Church, will be His Heavenly Bride, and of course will have access to this earth and dwell upon it, but Israel will be particularly God's earthly people during the eternal ages.

399. Where would you place Ezekiel, chapters 38 and 39, in their chronological sequence in the events of the "last days"?

In Ezekiel, chapter 36, we have a prophecy concerning the scattering and dispersion of Israel, and also the re-gathering back into the Land. In the 37th chapter we have this truth illustrated in the vision of the dry bones and the sign of the two sticks. In chapter 38 we have the invasion of the Russian armies against Palestine during the Tribulation after the Rapture of the Church, and in chapter 39 we have the judgment of God as He destroys the northern army, and re-establishes Israel in the Land during the Millennium. You will notice that the 39th chapter of Ezekiel ends with a picture of Israel safely settled in the Land of Palestine. (Read Ezekiel 39:25-29.)

400. What is the purpose of the Millennium?

Concerning the purpose of the Millennium, I feel that God is going to ultimately prove that man is absolutely unable to govern himself. He is going to allow him to try and solve the world's problems, until finally he comes to the end of his rope; and then the Lord will intervene, and set up His government and His Kingdom here upon the earth, to prove that the only stable and abiding government is that of the Lord Jesus Christ.

401. Will you inform me where the Bible teaching is given about the political and religious federations of the last days?

Concerning the Bible teaching about the political and

religious federation of the last days, I would especially refer you to the 17th and 18th chapters of the Book of Revelation. Here we find the final world federation—"the scarlet woman of Babylon," which we believe will be headed up by the Roman Catholic Church. Personally, I believe that this attempt to establish one worldwide religious and political organization began way back in the 11th chapter of Genesis with the building of the Tower of Babel through Nimrod. It has been the dream of the nations ever since, to have one great world united nations organization; and in order to effect this there would have to be one religion, because the differences of the various religious groups are the greatest obstacle to bringing the nations together.

Today we see this being fulfilled before our eyes, as the United Nations is seeking to unite all of the world under one organization, with a single world bank, and a United Nations army, together with a united educational and religious program. The presence of the National Council of Churches and the World Council of Churches today is already a step in the direction of this great world church. On every hand the line of demarcation between fundamentalism and modernism is being wiped out, and under the guise of tolerance even such movements as Seventh-day Adventism are given the right hand of fellowship by certain evangelicals.

All of this was foreshadowed in the Book of Daniel where the image was set up, and everyone was commanded to bow down to worship it upon pain of death. In the end time we believe too that the Antichrist, after the Church has been raptured, will cause all men to bow down and worship the beast, according to the prophecy of Revelation 13:13-18. It will become increasingly more difficult for those who stand firmly on the fundamentals of the faith and will not compromise with evil, to carry on, but we know that the God of the three young men who kept them in the fiery furnace in the days of Daniel is able to keep His own today as well.

402. Is there anything in Scripture which speaks of the sending of rockets to the moon? Do you think the Lord will ever allow that to happen? I would just like to have your opinion on this in the light of the Scriptures.

I do not know of any particular passage in the Bible which speaks definitely of these things, except that there will be signs in the sun and the moon, and fearful sights in the sky. Undoubtedly it has reference to what is going on now. Then too, in the 11th chapter of Genesis, men tried to build a tower which would reach into the heavens. Here we have the first effort of man to explore the heavens, and it may be a prophecy of what is happening right today. As it was in the days of old, so it will be again, and we believe that all these things are a sure indication of the soon return of the Lord Jesus Christ. How far the Lord will let man go we do not know, but we do know that before he comes to the ultimate of his own destruction, the Lord is going to step in and "he that shall come will come, and will not tarry" (Hebrew 10:37). What a blessing to know that we who belong to Him shall be spared from the awful time of Tribulation.

403. Do you believe that any of the latest implements for war will be used while the Church is on earth?

It is impossible to state when the modern weapons of war will be used. I personally feel that the coming

of the Lord is so close at hand, that these instruments
are being prepared for the Tribulation. I believe that
this interplanetary travel which is planned by Russia
and has caused such panic in the United States is a sign
of the end of the age. It was the original sin of Satan in
Isaiah 14 when he too said that he would ascend above
the clouds, and set his throne above the heavens. This
was the dream of Satan in the beginning, and God of
course intervened and cast him out. We believe that
the same thing is going to happen again, that the Lord
will let it go just so far and then will step in, and that
may be any day.

404. What is meant by "Jacob's trouble"?

This expression is found in Jeremiah 30:7,

> Alas! for that day is great, so that none is like it: it is
> even the time of JACOB'S TROUBLE, but he shall be
> saved out of it (Jer. 30:7).

The context clearly indicates it is the Tribulation,
the Day of the Lord. The word "Jacob" in this connection does not refer to him personally, but the nation
which sprang from him. It is a common expression in
the Bible to refer to the Nation of Israel as "Jacob" and
"Judah" also. It is in this connection that Jacob will
pass through the Tribulation, not personally, for he is
already with the Lord, but his descendants who will
then be upon the earth.

405. If the dead in Christ are already with the Lord, how can they rise first at the Rapture?

Concerning the "dead in Christ" at the Second Coming of our Lord, you must remember that at death the
SOUL goes to God in Heaven, while the BODY goes
into the grave. When Jesus comes He will bring these

souls with Him (I Thessalonians 4:14). Then these souls which come with the Lord Jesus Christ will be united to their resurrection bodies and then together caught up to meet the Lord in the air.

406. Who will reign over Israel—David or Christ?

They both will. Christ will reign over all the earth, including Israel, but David will be king under Christ over the Nation of Israel. The apostles will be under David judging the twelve tribes. See Ezekiel 34:23, 24; Ezekiel 37:24, 25; and Hosea 3:5.

CHAPTER XVI

RESURRECTION

407. How do you get a Sunday resurrection and teach a Wednesday crucifixion with a full (no more or no less) 72 hours in the heart of the earth?

To answer the question of how we can fit in the 72 hours or three days and three nights between Wednesday afternoon and the beginning of the first day of the week, you must remember that the Bible distinctly says:

> For as Jonas was three days and three nights in the whale's belly; so shall the Son of man be three days and three nights IN THE HEART OF THE EARTH (Matt. 12:40).

This does not mean that there would be three days and three nights, or 72 hours, pass between His death and His resurrection, but this was to be the time that He was to be in the tomb.

Since we know that the Lord Jesus Christ died at 3:00 o'clock in the afternoon, and that some time must have elapsed between that and His actual burial, it is reasonable to assume that Nicodemus and Joseph of Arimathea must have buried the Lord Jesus Christ at about sunset on Wednesday evening, and He arose immediately after sunset on Saturday, which of course was the beginning of Sunday, since days were then reckoned from sundown to sundown.

I think that the whole difficulty arises from the fact that we figure from the death of our Lord to His resurrection, whereas the Bible predicted that it would be from His BURIAL until His resurrection.

408. We would like your opinion on the statement that the resurrection was not on Sunday.

Concerning the day of the resurrection, there is no proof at all in the Bible that the Lord Jesus Christ arose on any other day but the first day of the week. If we remember that the first day of the week began immediately after sundown of the seventh day (approximately 6 o'clock on our Saturday), there is no difficulty. While the Lord was crucified on our Wednesday, and buried the same day, He arose at sundown or very shortly thereafter, on the first day of the week (as time was then reckoned).

There is not a verse in the Bible which says that the Lord Jesus Christ arose on the seventh day, and it is out of harmony with all the other teaching of the Word. The exact time of day is not given, but we are told that when the women came early in the morning while it was yet dark, Christ had already arisen; and so it is clear that the resurrection took place early on the first day of the week. The Saturday resurrection theory is another of the Seventh-day Adventist attempts to bolster their legalistic seventh-day error.

409. I am puzzled concerning the expression "three days and three nights," relating to the time Christ was in the grave, and the phrase "He arose on the third day." Do they refer to equal periods of time? To me there seems to be a difference. How do you explain this?

The Bible does say that Jesus was in the grave three

days and three nights, and it is also said that He arose the "third day." You must remember that the Bible also plainly states that the Lord was to rise AFTER three days and three nights in the tomb. In Matthew 27:63 we are definitely told that He would arise after three days:

> ...After three days I will rise again (Matt. 27:63).

This same statement is repeated again in Mark 8:31,

> And he began to teach them, that the Son of man must suffer many things, and be rejected of the elders, and of the chief priests, and scribes, and be killed, and AFTER THREE DAYS rise again (Mark 8:31).

Both the expressions "three days" and "third day" refer to the same length of time. We have another example of this in the Book of Esther, chapter 4. We read that Esther was not to eat or drink for three days, night or day, which of course would be three nights and three days. Then in Esther 5, verse 1, we read:

> Now it came to pass on the THIRD DAY, that Esther put on her royal apparel, and stood in the inner court of the king's house (Esther 5:1).

There the THIRD DAY meant "after three days and three nights." I believe, therefore, that there is no difficulty whatsoever, but only different expressions of the same length of time.

410. In the New Testament Christ says that He is the "firstfruits of the resurrection." How could Jonah have been resurrected, if that be true?

We believe that all those that were resurrected before the resurrection of Christ, died again. It was really, therefore, not so much a resurrection as a "temporary revival." Jonah as a type of the Lord Jesus Christ was brought back from the dead, as were also others. However, we believe that since Christ is the firstfruits, these "revived ones" died again and will be subsequently resurrected, never to perish any more.

The question of how Jonah could have been resurrected if Christ is the firstfruits, is the same problem which also arises with the resurrection of the young man of Nain, and the little maiden, as well as Lazarus in John, chapter 11. These evidently all died again later. They may have been in the resurrected company after Jesus' resurrection as recorded in Matthew 27:51-53.

411. Do we sleep in death until the Lord comes, or are born-again Christians taken to be with the Lord when they die? I am so confused on the teaching of "soul sleep."

The Bible is very clear that when a Christian dies his body goes into the grave, but his soul goes consciously into the presence of the Lord. Jesus said to the thief on the cross, "To day shalt thou be with me in paradise" (Luke 23:43). Certainly this does not refer to soul sleeping. In II Corinthians 5 Paul tells us that to be absent from the body is to be present with the Lord (II Cor. 5:8). From these and other Scriptures there is no question in my mind but that when we as believers die, we go immediately to be with the Lord. Then when the Lord Jesus Christ comes for His Church, the sleeping bodies will be resurrected and joined to their souls, and then caught up together with all believers in the air, to meet the Lord (read I Thessalonians 4:13-18).

CHAPTER XVII

SEGREGATION AND INTEGRATION

412. What is the Bible answer to the race problem and the idea of a completely integrated society?

The race problem is not a difficult one for me to answer, since I do not believe that the Bible teaches a completely integrated society. I believe we must recognize the fact that the Bible warns us against the "unequal yoke," which means that we are not to advocate marriage between believers and unbelievers, but also between people whose background and nationality are so incompatible that there is no hope of a happy union. I believe that God has divided the various races for a purpose. This is very graphically illustrated in the strict rules of separation which the Lord gave to Israel, forbidding them to have any relationship of integration with the Gentiles. Their worship and diet and customs were all designed to keep them a separate people. While I believe that we ought to treat all races alike, and give them every opportunity, without showing any favoritism, I do not believe in the intermarriage of those races which are so different temperamentally and emotionally that there is no hope of any blessing.

413. What should our attitude as Christians be concerning school integration?

The matter of racial integration in the schools is a difficult problem which presents many different angles depending on local circumstances and conditions, so that a general rule covering all areas and situations cannot be laid down. For this reason I believe that the Supreme Court order forcing the integration was unfortunate and ill-timed. I believe the court acted prematurely in seeking to effect integration by law and force. It is not with me a question of the "right" or "wrong" of school integration, as much as a question of expediency and good judgment.

I personally believe that the business of integration should have been left to the local authorities. We cannot apply one rule to all the different sections of the nation without regard to local conditions. Some communities, and even states, may not be ready for the sudden change, while others may present no problem at all. The issue should be settled on the merits of the particular situation in each locality. I therefore believe it was an error to have the court take this action at this particular time. The time was not ripe for such a drastic move. Great progress was being made by the southern states, and a little more time would have solved the question without stirring up all this violence and hatred. We cannot doubt the sincerity of the proponents of integration; but while progress was being made, I believe the saying should have been followed, "let sleeping dogs lie," and "leave good enough alone."

However, it is the law now, and we must "be subject to the powers that be" (Rom. 13:1), and an effort should be made to obey the law of the land as far as possible without violence and hatred.

414. What is the difference in the blood of a negro and a white man?

There is no difference, for God hath "made of one

blood all nations of men for to dwell on all the face of the earth" (Acts 17:26). There is only one kind of human blood—the blood of sinful father Adam, so "there is no difference: For all have sinned" (Rom. 3:22, 23).

415. Do you believe in racial segregation or in integration?

The answer to this question is both YES and NO. On one plane of life I believe in segregation, while on other planes I do not. The answer is not simple, for we must consider it from at least four different angles.

1. SPIRITUALLY, there is no such thing as segregation. All believers are one in Christ Jesus, no matter what their color or nationality. In this we make no difference. We consider every believer as a brother in Christ, regardless of color.

2. INDUSTRIALLY, we believe that segregation is wrong. No one should be denied an opportunity for work or advancement because of nationality or color. However, for "social" reasons (see 4 below) it may at times be more advisable for them to work with those of their own color, nationality, or social standing.

3. EDUCATIONALLY, we believe that everyone should have equal opportunity to obtain an education. Where there is a small minority of another race, there is no other way but to mix the races. However, where there are sufficient numbers of the different classes, so that several buildings are needed, it may be a happier solution if they can gather with others who have common backgrounds and surroundings. We believe that local conditions should determine these matters.

4. SOCIALLY, we are faced with a different problem. Social integration carries the gravest dangers. I definitely do not believe in the intermarriage of Negroes and

Whites. This is not because of discrimination, but is a matter of expedience and common sense. The temperament, background, habits, and sentiments of the two are so diverse as to make for misunderstanding and unhappiness. I do not believe in the intermarriage of Catholics and Protestants, not because I discriminate against the Catholics, but common sense teaches that if they both "stick to their religion" it will be a divided home. The same is true of Baptists and Pentecostalists: Their views are so wide apart that there is little likelihood of agreement and a happy family. For this same reason I feel Negroes and Whites should never intermarry, but where possible live in their own social and religious groups and churches.

We choose our friends from among those with whom we have the most in common, and as there is so little in common among some groups, integration is definitely a step in the wrong direction.

416. Why are the negroes still black after being some generations in a more temperate climate like the United States?

The change in color from white to black did not take place in one or two generations, but over a period of thousands of years. If the colored people remain in this northern temperate zone as many generations as it took for them to become black, I am of the firm opinion that they would begin to bleach out in time too, and their skin would become white. You must remember that the colored people have been in this country only a relatively short time as compared with the many generations that they have lived in Africa.

417. Do you believe that negroes and whites should live mixed in the same community. Would there be any reference in God's word which would give us the correct answer?

This is one of the most frequent questions asked. I repeat, therefore, what I have said many times: I have my serious doubts about the advisability of pushing this matter as it seems to be done by our government. I do not feel that we ought to hold anything against the Negroes at all, and that we should give them every opportunity for their own social life, within their own circle and business opportunities; but as far as the intimate relationship and fellowship which comes by living in the same sections in a community, I do not believe that the time is ripe.

We realize that when Negroes are saved they are members of the Body of Christ, just the same as other folk, but we also recognize that there is a great social difference between them which will undoubtedly take many generations to wipe out. I therefore look with a great deal of suspicion upon the growing trend of wiping out all of these racial lines as far as social intercourse is concerned.

As far as I know, there is no Scripture which would bear directly upon this particular problem.

418. I heard you say in one of your messages that "there is no superior race." Do you mean by this that all men are on an equal social level?

I am afraid that you misunderstood me. I did not in any way mean to advocate social equality between the races. I realize that this is quite impossible under present conditions. I was merely speaking about the fact that the BLOOD in all the races of humanity is identically the same, and there is no difference. They are all sinners before God, and need to be saved by the blood of the Lord Jesus Christ.

I certainly do not feel that we should give such complete social equality to the colored people as to encourage intermarriage among the races. I am sure that you will agree with me that they should be given the Gospel. They should also be given equal opportunity, and every social and educational opportunity wherever this does not involve an intermingling socially in the matter of marriage.

SUBJECT INDEX

269

SCRIPTURE REFERENCE INDEX

HOW TO USE:
    This Scripture Reference Index has been arranged to help you make effective use of the book. The books of the Bible are arranged chronologically, with the chapter or verse reference indicated, along with the question number which deals with this particular passage. For example, if you are interested in Matthew, chapter 7, you will find under "Matthew" that verses 21 to 23 are discussed in questions #183, #223, and #291.